WHERE COYOTES HOWL AND WIND BLOWS FREE

WHERE COYOTES HOWL

Edited by Alexandra R. Haslam
and Gerald W. Haslam

ND WIND BLOWS FREE

GROWING UP IN THE WEST

 University of Nevada Press

Reno   Las Vegas

The paper used in this book meets the requirements of American National Standard for Information Sciences—Permanence of Paper for Printed Library Materials, ANSI Z39.48-1984. Binding materials were selected for strength and durability.

Library of Congress Cataloging-in-Publication Data

Where coyotes howl and wind blows free : growing up in the West /
    edited by Alexandra R. Haslam and Gerald W. Haslam
        p.   cm.
    Summary: A collection of stories, folktales, legends, and essays
    set in the American West.
    Includes bibliographical references (p.   ).
    ISBN 0-87417-255-1
    1. West (U.S.)—Literary collections. [1. West (U.S.)—Literary
    collections.]   I. Haslam, Alexandra R., 1963–   II. Haslam,
    Gerald W.
    PZ5.W5245   1995
    810.8'03278—dc20   94-38567
                                                                   CIP
                                                                    AC

Cover illustration from the lithograph, *Howl,* by Luis Jimenez
University of Nevada Press, Reno, Nevada 89557 USA
Copyright © 1995 by University of Nevada Press

Book design by Erin Kirk New
Printed in the United States of America

10 09 08 07 06 05 04 03 02   5 4 3 2

In memory of Wally Stegner and Fred Manfred,
two good guys . . .

CONTENTS

Prologue by Wilma Elizabeth McDaniel   ix
Introduction   xi

Deepest Roots

Okanogan (traditional)   *Creation of the Animal People*   3
Jo Bender   *Coyote and Bullfish*   5
Skye Mitchell   *Rolling Head*   7
Darryl Babe Wilson   *Hunting and Fishing*   10

Settlement, Legend, and Myth

Arnold R. Rojas   *Varmints*   17
Zilpha Keatley Snyder   *The Three Men*   20
Robert Laxalt   *Basque Hotel*   30
Rudolfo Anaya   *The Golden Carp*   38

Rural Lives

Wallace Stegner   *A Frontier Boyhood*   51
Levi Peterson   *The Newsboy*   57

Wilma Elizabeth McDaniel   *Recognition of an Artist*   74

Captives   76

Robert Franklin Gish   *Blue Danube Waltz*   78
Cyra McFadden   *Rodeo Life*   86
Louis Owens   *Water Witch*   92

Growth of Community

Dorothy Bryant   *The New Sidewalk*   101
Gerald W. Haslam   *Mal de Ojo*   109
Jeanne Wakatsuki Houston   *Papa's Holiday Spirit*   118
Rafael Zepeda   *Peato*   121
Mary Helen Ponce   *Cousin Mandy*   125
Genny Lim   *A Juk-Sing Opera*   131

New Experience, Old Wisdom

Chitra Banerjee Divakaruni   *Grocery Shopping with Aunt Geeta*   141
Hisaye Yamamoto   *Dried Snakeskins*   146
Clark Brown   *The Way West*   149
Bao-Tran Truong   *Stepping Stones in America*   152
Maxine Hong Kingston   *Reparation Candy*   157

Urban Encounters

Gary Soto   *Being Mean*   163
Jess Mowry   *Animal Rights . . .*   168
Mee Her   *Bowling to Find a Lost Father*   174
Wanda Coleman   *The Seamstress*   177
John H. Irsfeld   *School Days*   180
Richard Brautigan   *Funeral Child*   188
James D. Houston   *Elegy*   192

Epilogue by Marek Breiger   197
Credits   199

PROLOGUE

OLD NEIGHBOR REPORTS ON A TRIP TO MERCED

Wilma Elizabeth McDaniel

> Everything has changed
> he lamented
> > nothing like the old Merced
> > drive out any direction
> > all the new houses
> > big air base at Winton
> > strange faces
>
> Oh, now and then you will see
> > an old Portugee ranch
> > with a tankhouse
> > and pomegranate bushes
> > in the yard
> > but don't expect it to be the
> > same
>
> and all them little kids playin'
> > in the dust
> > ain't Okies now
> > they call 'em boat people

INTRODUCTION

We are from cities and suburbs. And ranches. And farms.
And villages. We live in house trailers and mansions and
apartments and tents. We are red and black and yellow and
white and brown. Increasingly, we are mixtures. We are
female and male.

We are westerners, and these stories—fiction and nonfiction—all seek truth. They reveal that, no matter what
our color or sex, we have more uniting us than separating
us. What is most important is that we are all members of
the human family.

Our native region isn't necessarily what people have
imagined. Despite the images projected by movies and
popular novels, the American West remains diverse and
dynamic. The great cities of the West, like Los Angeles
and Dallas, Denver and Seattle, suffer all the urban problems and offer all the urban advantages found elsewhere.
But the West also retains vast stretches of open land—of
forests, of deserts, of waterways—even some wilderness.
Nevertheless, a great many westerners live in towns that
could be located anywhere.

Any two people who have grown up in this region will not necessarily have had the same experiences. Not everyone is a cowboy—in fact, very few people are—just as not everyone is white. Not everyone is a surfer or a gang member or a farmer or a movie star, either. We are simply people, living.

Some of us have come from tumbleweed families that move from place to place. Others of us have lived in the houses where our great-grandparents were born. Still others have had no houses at all.

The ancestors of some of us were here before the first pale-skinned people arrived. Some of us arrived only yesterday . . . from Southeast Asia or Central America or Eastern Europe . . . continuing the process of building America.

What the West has offered is considerable open space, much aridity, and the rough blending of diverse ethnic groups and cultures. And it has offered hope—or the hope of hope—so a great many poor people, often immigrants, have come here seeking work for themselves and opportunities for their children. Some have achieved their goals, even prosperity. But the odds have not always been even, because racism and discrimination and environmental exploitation have historically been tolerated here. The West is by no means perfect.

Our varied, imposing landscapes offer an awareness of nature, its imperatives and its losses: How can one *not* notice the Rocky Mountains? The Sonora Desert? The coast of Oregon? The plains of Texas? The high prairie of Wyoming? The Great Central Valley of California? How can one *not* ask questions: Where will desert cities like Los Angeles, Las Vegas, and Phoenix find their water as they continue expanding? What will be the long-term consequences of decades of pesticides and other toxins applied to western landscapes? How long will some of us continue tolerating bigotry or discrimination just because we are not its victims? How long will we continue abusing this fragile land?

Yet by no means is everything negative. Many settings here retain a natural grandeur unknown elsewhere.

Here, too, many immigrants have mixed to create a new society and even new kinds of people. Notice how many of the writers in this book are ethnic mixtures—unabashedly *part* Hispanic or *part* African or *part*

Indian and, of course, *all* American. In reality, we westerners are all blends—all part Hispanic, all part African, all part Indian, and so on—because our society combines elements of all its parts: we have cultural if not genetic roots extending to every continent.

And this, our western realm, remains the focus of limitless, sometimes unrealistic yearnings worldwide: it is the place where many, many people believe life can be better.

For us, though, it is the place where most of us were born and raised, the place we have chosen to live and, perhaps, to die.

It is home.

Alexandra R. and Gerald W. Haslam
Penngrove, California

DEEPEST ROOTS

"Earth is alive yet, but she has been changed."

CREATION OF THE ANIMAL PEOPLE

OKANOGAN (TRADITIONAL)

The earth was once a human being. Old-One made her out of a woman. "You will be the mother of all people," he said.

Earth is alive yet, but she has been changed. The soil is her flesh; the rocks are her bones; the wind is her breath; trees and grass are her hair. She lives spread out, and we live on her. When she moves, we have an earthquake.

After changing her to earth, Old-One took some of her flesh and rolled it into balls, as people do with mud or clay. These balls Old-One made into the beings of the early world. They were the ancients. They were people, and yet they were at the same time animals.

In form, some of them were like animals; some were more like people. Some could fly like birds; others could swim like fishes. In some ways the land creatures acted like animals. All had the gift of speech. They had greater powers and were more cunning than either animals or people. And yet they were very stupid in some ways. They knew that they had to hunt in order to live, but they did not know which beings were deer and which were people. They thought people were deer and often ate them.

Some people lived on the earth at that time. They were like the Indians of today except that they were ignorant. Deer also were on the earth at that time. They were real animals then too. They were never people or ancient animal people, as were the ancestors of most animals. Some people say that elk, antelope, and buffalo also were always animals, to be hunted as deer are hunted. Others tell stories about them as if they were ancients or half-human beings.

The last balls of mud Old-One made were almost all alike and were different from the first ones he made. He rolled them over and over. He shaped them like Indians. He blew on them and they became alive. Old-One called them men. They were Indians, but they were very ignorant. They did not know how to do things. They were the most helpless of all creatures Old-One made. Some of the animal people preyed on them and ate them.

Old-One made both male and female people and animals, so that they might breed and multiply. Thus all living things came from the earth. When we look around, we see everywhere parts of our mother.

Most of the ancient animal people were selfish, and there was much trouble among them. At last Old-One said, "There will soon be no people if I let things go on like this."

So he sent Coyote to kill all the monsters and other evil beings. Old-One told Coyote to teach the Indians the best way to do things and the best way to make things. Life would be easier and better for them when they were no longer ignorant. Coyote then traveled on the earth and did many wonderful things.

This is a traditional tale from the Okanogan culture of Washington and British Columbia. All cultures have tales to explain human existence— the Judeo-Christian version is called Genesis—and all acknowledge that there are powers beyond human control. This creation story, which was passed on by oral tale-tellers, accounts for human life in sacred terms. It offers a glimpse into the heart and mind of a unique American culture.

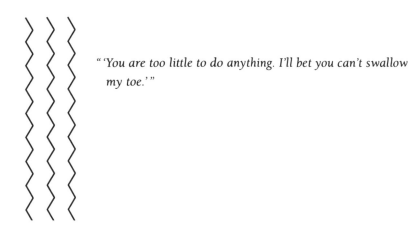

*" 'You are too little to do anything. I'll bet you can't swallow
my toe.' "*

COYOTE AND BULLFISH

JO BENDER

Coyote was going up the river to visit someone. He was
very well dressed. He had his quiver, bow and arrows,
moccasins, and beads. He looked very fine. It was a hot
summer day. He came to a nice stretch of sand. He saw
Bullfish sunning himself. He was black as charcoal. Coyote
said, "What are you doing there?"

Bullfish didn't say a word. Coyote talked and talked
but Bullfish never answered. At last Coyote said, "You are
pretty small. You are too little to do anything. I'll bet you
can't swallow my toe," and at the same time he thrust his
toe in front of Bullfish's mouth. Bullfish just turned his
head away.

Then Coyote said, "I'll give you my bow and arrows if
you bite me." He teased Bullfish that way for a long time.
Finally Bullfish nipped Coyote's toe. Coyote did not pay
any attention to him; he only continued to taunt him.
Soon Bullfish had swallowed Coyote's leg; Coyote became
frightened and begged for mercy, but Bullfish ignored
him and kept on swallowing him. Coyote offered him all

his fine things, but Bullfish just swallowed him entirely and swam off under a rock in the riffle.

The people missed Coyote. They hunted for him and found his valuables on the sand and saw the track where he had been dragged in. So they asked a doctor to find out where he was. The doctor went into a trance and about in the middle of the night said that he was under the water, that Bullfish had swallowed him, but that he was not yet dead.

Then Bullfish made the water muddy so the people could not find him. Otter, Raccoon, everyone hunted for Coyote but they could not find him. At last Mud-Spear [a water bird] climbed a tree and looked. He said, "I see a tail under a rock in the riffle. I am going to try to spear him." So he took a spear pole, aimed carefully, and speared Bullfish right above the tail. The people pulled him out and cut open his abdomen. Coyote jumped out and said, "Nephew, I have been sleeping."

JO BENDER, a Wintu from the upper Sacramento River in northern California, recounted this traditional tale. Coyote, who as usual doesn't know when to quit, is a trickster figure, given to excesses of human appetites. As Malcolm Margolin points out, "he is a talented, never-tiring creator of his own downfall," so he gets himself into all sorts of trouble, and rarely admits a mistake. Some other tricksters important in American culture are Anansi the spider from Africa and Reynard the fox from Europe. Tales about tricksters tend to be instructive, even cautionary—even if all they teach is "Don't act like this jerk."

"Then her head alone was left and rolled about. She went rolling over the ground, her sister still beside her."

ROLLING HEAD

SKYE MITCHELL

Long ago people came into being and lived at a village; it was filled with people. People lived both on the flat on the west side of the river and on the flat on the east side of the river too. There was a chief at the head of the people who had two daughters. The younger one reached puberty, but she did not tell her mother. However, her parents knew it. So they were to call a puberty dance, and they met and discussed it. In the evening the father spoke. "Early in the morning go strip bark for a maple bark apron," he said. "But don't take the girl who has reached puberty with you. Go secretly," he said.

The rest of the women got up early in the morning. They all went secretly; quite a little way north they went, and even some went north uphill and crossed the ridge to the north. Then later she woke up, the one who had reached puberty. And she went, though she was forbidden to go she went, going behind the others. She kept going until she reached them. Some were stripping bark and others already had much. She went right up to them and cut off maple bark.

All at once, she stuck her little finger with a splinter. It bled. Her older sister came up to her and wiped it with dead leaves. Then they said, "When will it leave off? The blood cannot stop flowing." And the rest of them left, they knew already and were afraid so they left. She and her older sister were left behind alone. Some who had already gone reached the house and told the father. "She got stuck with a splinter while stripping bark," they said. And the old man said, "She does not listen to me."

She who had reached puberty, who was downhill to the north, now sucked blood and spat it out. Then more blood came and though she sucked the blood she could not stop its flow. Meanwhile the sun began to set. Until early evening she sucked, she kept on sucking, not being able to help herself. Then she got tired, not being able to stop it in any way. Suddenly she happened to swallow blood and smelled the fat. It tasted sweet. So now she ate her little finger, she ate it, and then ate her whole hand. Then she ate both her hands, devoured them. Then she ate her leg, ate both her legs. Then she ate up her whole body. Then her head alone was left and rolled about. She went rolling over the ground, her sister still beside her.

The old man in the house said, "From the north she'll come, she who went to strip maple bark. Put on your clothes, people. Get your weapons. We people are gone." And the people dressed themselves and got their weapons. And from the north they saw her come, she came rolling toward the house. She arrived in the early evening and lay there. After she had stayed there a while, she bounced up to the west across the river to the flat on the west, where she threw the people into her mouth. She did not linger, she turned the village upside down as she devoured them all. Then she fell to the east across the river and lay there, and the next morning she threw those of the east flat into her mouth, ate them, devoured them all. Only her eldest sister she left for a while. And she went about the world, and when she saw people she threw them into her mouth and ate them. Each evening she came home, each morning she went about the world looking for people. Always she went searching.

One day she climbed up to the northern edge of the sky and looked all over the world, but she saw no one. So in the evening she came home, and the next morning she got up and threw her elder sister into her mouth. Then she came on her way, until she reached the edge of a big creek. She did not know how to cross. And from the other side she called. A man was sitting there. He threw a bridge over from the other side. She was crossing, and when she had gone halfway he jerked it, and it went down at Talat. And she fell into the river, and as she fell into the water a riffle pike jumped and swallowed her. And it is finished. That is all.

SKYE MITCHELL, also Wintu but from the McCloud River branch of that tribe, recounted this menstruation tale. A major event in any young woman's life, menstruation was believed to give her magical powers, but it was also seen as negative, even unclean in some cultures. Pubescent girls usually underwent an important ritual of maturation. In fact, because monthly periods were understood as much in supernatural as natural terms, most cultures placed restrictions on women during those times. The important point, however, is that girls had become capable of bearing children, a process that remains mysterious and magical.

*"Deer came to drink as we sat quietly. They simply appeared—
their huge ears ever alert, their tails twitching, the yearlings
dancing."*

HUNTING AND FISHING

DARRYL BABE WILSON

Before lunch we were on one arm of Lake Britton. It was
both sunny and shady there, warm and cool. We fished
silently for a long time. I was impatient with the results
and kept wanting to pull in the line and check the worm.
Daddy cautioned me to be quiet. Without even a whisper a flock of canvasback ducks, their brown-red heads
all pointed in the same direction, floated by us, parting
the mirror surface of the lake. They slipped around some
tules. Their ripples on the lake's surface vanished. I wondered if they were really there or if they were a part of my
imagination.

Very slowly our fishing line moved. Daddy said, "Pull er
in!" I pulled. There was no give. There was no fighting. I
pulled harder. Whatever it was, it wasn't coming up very
fast! I pulled again and soon tired of the operation. Daddy
took the fishing pole and grabbed the line. He pulled long,
hard, and slow. Whatever it was moved towards us very
slowly. "Must be an old limb," Daddy said. Up it came.
Slowly, slowly, slowly . . . It was close now. Then, out of
the depths floated a huge, light-brown turtle, the worm

still dangling from its hawklike beak. Its little eyes blinked, and its paws
clawed awkwardly to get away.

We wrestled "Mr. Turtle" out of the water. "Careful! If he snaps you
he might cut your finger clear off." I jumped far back, one hand holding
the other, thinking that I would rather have all of my fingers for the
rest of my life. "Can we eatem?" I asked. "Um humm" was the reply. We
didn't. Daddy etched the date on Mr. Turtle's shell with his knife, then
turned him loose. We left for an "undisturbed" fishing hole.

Deer came to drink as we sat quietly. They simply appeared—their huge
ears ever alert, their tails twitching, the yearlings dancing. Daddy used
slight head and eye gestures to point out the variety of life surrounding
us. High in the blue, buzzards lazily turned. Over in the mirror lake's
silver, an osprey swooped down, hit the sleeping surface with a violent
splash, emerged from the splash before the exploded water began arch-
ing back to earth. Powerful wings flapping, it moved slowly skyward
with a huge, desperately flopping, silver fish. I watched in amazement.
It seems I was amazed at almost everything.

It would be more than a week before the rest of the family would join
us, so Daddy decided not to kill a deer—because we could not eat it
all and a lot of it might spoil unless we took the time to cut it in small
strips and dry it. We didn't have enough time. We "mucked out" the
old house, throwing piles of trash out the back door. Daddy hammered
boards back into place. We attempted to fix the windows. The door
hinges were rusty and the boards were rotting away. We managed to
find some lumber in the barn that was protected from the weather. We
used it to fix up the old house. For two days we burned piles of debris.
Next, we mucked out the old spring and cleaned the ditch so the water
would run from the spring to the house.

Soon we had running water—at least to within twenty feet of the
front door! Next we planted potatoes. We cut the potatoes into four or
five parts, dropped them along the furrows, then covered them with the
dirt turned by the now shining plow. All we had to do was wait to eat.
The wait would only be until autumn. . . .

We hammered and banged and sawed, patching up the old barn. I am sure that we disturbed the owls, the snakes, the lizards, and the bats, but we had to get the place ready for the livestock and the family. Our old car came lurching down the hill. It stopped, reluctantly. Kids exploded from the doors and windows—curiosity being their guide, my brothers and sisters scrambled in every direction.

Since all of the family was together again, it was time to go hunting. Daddy and me slept in the barn under the hay. This, he said, was because the smell of the hay would camouflage our body odor. Then he said to sleep and dream about the deer, to *see* them in my dreams as we would see them in the morning. I slept. I dreamed. I *saw*.

Long before daylight we were off towards the lake. The deer would be drinking about daybreak, and Daddy wanted to be in place before they arrived. We stopped once in the early shadows to crush skunk berries and skunk berry leaves in our hands and wipe the juice over our clothing and into our hair. This was for more camouflage.

We nestled there in the darkness beside the lake and beside the deer trail for a long, long time. A sensing within Daddy caused me to come alert. I strained to see in the soft darkness in the deep shadows of the towering pines. Then! There it was, the deer I *saw* in my dream! My spirit screamed, "Shoot! Shoot!" Daddy waited. The deer slowly vanished. Another deer slid into view. "Shoot!" my spirit screamed. Silence. That deer slid away into the shadows. Deer after deer appeared, then vanished. Finally, when I least expected it, "BOOM!"

The silence in the forest shattered, the report lashed across the surface of the lake and bounced from tree to tree in the thick forest. All but one of the deer vanished. Daddy opened the stomach of the deer, placed the head of the deer to the west and its tail to the east. He took out the entrails and found the liver. The purple liver shined in the early light. It still had blood dripping from it. Daddy cut off a piece of that liver and ate it. He then cut off a piece for me. I ate it, not liking the taste or not liking the circumstances. But, it was a part of our ritual—a way of asking forgiveness for shattering the silence, for committing the crime of murdering the deer, and for interfering with the other forces of life that we can know so little of.

Tying its four legs together so he could carry it on his shoulders, Daddy carried the deer home. With some arrogance, I carried the rifle. We feasted that night. *Spot-le* (fried potatoes), *wa-hatch* (pan bread) and *dose me-suts* (fried deer meat).

DARRYL BABE WILSON is a member of the Fall River Modoc tribe. He has developed a strong reputation as storyteller, a writer, and a poet who has not abandoned his ancestral heritage. He is presently completing a Ph.D. at the University of Arizona. "Hunting and Fishing" is excerpted from a longer memoir, "*Haya-Wa Atwan (Porcupine Valley)*."

SETTLEMENT, LEGEND, AND MYTH

"The firing squad was abolished. From then on, men who were condemned to death were locked up in the 'Celda Del Alacran' (scorpion cell)."

VARMINTS

ARNOLD R. ROJAS

The vaqueros with whom I rode in my youth came from many origins and often had interesting backgrounds. The stories about their early life always fascinated me and kept me around the embers of the campfire when I should have been in my blankets, sleeping. This is a story told me by a vaquero who rode on the great Terrazazas Haciendas in the state of Chihuahua, in old Mexico.

"Rattlers were not the only varmints which menaced us. In dry weather, scorpions and centipedes crawled out of the adobe walls of the houses we lived in. At night, as soon as we blew out the candle, we could hear them on the floor. They sounded like paper rustling. They would scurry into the dark whenever we lit a candle and we never put our feet on the floor in the dark, for fear of being stung.

"Here, one never comes in contact with scorpions or centipedes, unless one works in ditches, tunnels, or mines. But in my native town, we lived in adobe houses. Scorpions and centipedes live in the walls of all adobe houses. They were the poisonous variety, much smaller than the kind we find in California, which are not very poisonous. Those in the town where I was born had killed many people, especially children.

"There is a story told in a region where the scorpions are very poisonous; there was a cell in the city prison from which no man ever came out alive. After a series of deaths, the reason was discovered—a scorpion was the killer! Once this fact was established, the firing squad was discarded. From then on, men who were condemned to death were locked up in the 'Celda Del Alacran' (scorpion cell). The scorpion killer would sting the man while he slept. The poison was so deadly, death was instantaneous and thus eliminated the wastage of cartridges.

"The dusty little adobe town, where I was born, slept in the sun for most of the year, except when a cloudburst in the mountains would bring a *crescenta* (flood) roaring down the arroyo. The torrent would wash dens of snakes out of the hills, and when the water spread over the flat land on which the town was built, it would deposit hundreds of diamondback *joruba* (humpbacked) rattlers. They would infest the houses, sheds, and chicken houses.

"There would be an epidemic of snakebites among dogs. The snakes would give the inhabitants many frights before the hogs, which roamed the town and acted as scavengers, ate all the snakes.

"The only industry of the area was cattle raising, but the herds were small because it took leagues of desert range to support a cow. The people of the town were so poor that, when a couple were married, they were classified into those who would eat every day and those who would eat every other day.

"The cattle roaming the desert became very wild, and a vaquero from that desert country was very skillful in outwitting his charges. I wanted to escape this poverty, so I crossed the border into New Mexico. I found work there and was happy, chiefly because New Mexico fascinated me.

"Of all Hispanic peoples, those of New Mexico are the most friendly. They are also the most indifferent. They often never bother to learn English. In this respect, they are like the French, who do not try to learn a foreign language. In New Mexico, if one must speak, it must be Spanish or not at all.

"When the War came, the recruiting officers soon learned about this quirk of theirs and did not ask too many questions, but signed them up as soldiers. I went to the recruiting office and tried to enlist. I was not asked many questions and soon found myself in the army and before I knew it, I was in Germany. The officers assumed I was native-born. After the war, I got citizenship papers and came to California, where I went to work for Miller and Lux."

ARNOLD R. (CHIEF) ROJAS, the famous chronicler of vaqueros, was one of the Southwest's great storytellers. His Mexican roots were Yaqui, Mayo, and Sephardic, and he was all cowboy. Rojas's books recaptured the sense of the oral literary tradition, because he wrote the way vaqueros of his day actually told stories to one another, often wandering around a subject, but always pithy, and sometimes pulling the reader's leg. Good storytellers like Chief Rojas seldom allow facts to stand in the way of a yarn. Among his many books are *These Were the Vaqueros* (1974) and *Vaqueros and Buckaroos* (1979).

"Old Sally told Violet about things like ghosts and haunts and spirits, and all about the three men. And then Violet told Guy."

THE THREE MEN

ZILPHA KEATLEY SNYDER

Guy was way up in the pepper tree when the three men came over the ridge. He'd climbed up there right after he dropped Aunt's favorite platter because he needed time to decide what to do; whether to tell her and get it over with, or run away a year early. He'd always planned to wait until he was twelve, but then that heavy old platter that Aunt set such great store by had to go and slip out of his soapy hands. After he'd swept up the pieces and hid them in the ash pile he'd climbed the pepper tree. He cried some, but the wind that had been blowing all day long dried his tears before he could even taste them.

After a while he stopped crying and stretched out with his cheek on the prickly bark. He wrapped his arms and legs around the thick limb and hung on tightly while the Santa Ana, the hot, dry wind blowing in from the desert, dried his eyes and whisked long strands of pepper leaves, like thin prickly fingers, across his face and arms. Hanging on like that made him feel better. It wasn't that he was afraid of falling. It was just a good feeling to be almost a part of the solid old tree.

The sun had gone down and the sky behind the razorback ridge turned fiery red before Aunt came home from town. The first thing Guy heard was the clip clop of hooves, and for a moment he prayed that it might be Juliet, Uncle Joe's riding mare. But he might have known it wasn't. Uncle Joe had gone to the Gardners' to help with the new barn, and there was to be a shindig afterward that would probably last until late at night. Aunt had done a lot of yelling that morning when Uncle Joe said he was going to the barn raising. She'd said it was just like him to go off and waste a whole day helping riffraff like the Gardners while there was so much that needed doing right there on their own place.

Among a whole lot of other things, she'd also yelled that she was leaving. She was going off to Pasadena, she said, to live with her rich sister. But Guy hadn't gotten his hopes up. She was always saying that, and she never did go. But this time after Uncle Joe left, Aunt told Guy to harness up Old Jacob, and for a moment he'd wondered. But then she'd said she was only going into town to buy a length of dress goods. And now it was sunset, and the hooves in the driveway were Old Jacob's, and a few minutes later Guy heard the squeaky groan of the buggy as Aunt climbed out. Not long afterward she came out on the kitchen stoop and called.

"Guy! You Guy!" she yelled four or five times before she gave up and went back into the house. So far she was probably only wanting him to come take care of Old Jacob. She sounded angry but no more than usual, so she hadn't noticed the missing platter yet. Guy was thinking he had to hurry up and decide, and starting to cry all over again, when he looked up—and there they were.

There were three of them, and against the smoky red of the sky they looked as dark and crookedy as burnt matchsticks. They came slowly up above the horizon, their spiky elbows and knees bending like rusty hinges. They went on walking right up the ridge for a ways, jiggling along like puppet toys on a stage, before they started down through the high pasture. At first Guy was too busy worrying about Aunt and the platter to think much about them. It crossed his mind that they were probably some of the Jacksons on their way home from the Gardners' shindig. It took them a long time to disappear into the gully in the west fork and an even longer time to come back into sight on the other side, and in the meantime Guy had other things to think about.

Aunt came out again and yelled, and from in front of the house Guy could hear Old Jacob nickering and thumping the ground with a front hoof, eager to be taken to the barn and rubbed down and fed. Guy had almost forgotten about the three men, wondering what to do about Old Jacob and Aunt and the platter, when all of a sudden there they were again. Now that they were nearer and below the sunset he could see flutters of raggedy clothing and long gray wisps of hair that blew back from beneath the broad brims of their hats. Seeing them in the red-stained dusk and especially from behind a fringe of pepper leaves, a person might have taken them for road-weary travelers, or three old prospectors down from the high mountains. Guy might have climbed down from the tree and gone to meet them, if he hadn't remembered, all of a sudden, about something Violet had told him way back last winter.

Violet lived on a big rackety homestead in Dry Barranca Valley with George and Amelia Gardner, who were her father and mother. There'd been a lot of other flowers, Rose and Lily and maybe even Geranium and Petunia, but they'd all gotten married and left home before Violet was born. Aunt said the Gardners should have quit trying for George Herbert Gardner Junior after the fifth or sixth flower. Aunt said she'd told Amelia Gardner as much, right to her face. But according to Aunt, Amelia Gardner wasn't one to listen to well-meant advice, and they'd gone ahead and tried again for a boy. And all they got was Violet. Aunt said that Violet was what came of having a young'un when you were old enough to be its grandma. Aunt said Violet was loony.

Guy didn't know. He liked listening to Violet. Maybe it was loony and maybe it was plain fibbing, but whatever it was he liked hearing it. "Hey, Violet!" he'd yell when he saw her at recess or on her way to school, and she'd stop and wait for him, with her sparky eyes glittering and a secret smile tightening the corners of her mouth. "Hey," he'd say again and she'd start right in telling him one thing or another. Nothing Violet told him was like the kind of things most people talked about, but Guy didn't know if it was loony or not.

Some of it was about dragons. That was when Guy first started going to Barranca School after somebody wrote to the county (Aunt said it was probably Amelia Gardner that did it), and the truant officer came and had a long talk with Aunt. That year Guy and Violet and Nellie Anderson were the whole fourth grade, only Guy was ten already and would have been in the fifth if the truant officer had come sooner.

After the dragons it was unicorns for a while. Once when Aunt had gone into town, Guy had gone with Violet to look for one in the clearing near the Joneses' spring. He hadn't seen anything but an old hoof mark that looked like it might have been made by the Joneses' billygoat. But Violet had seen the unicorn. That's what she said, anyway.

But then, after Violet started visiting with Old Sally, she began to talk about other things besides unicorns and dragons. Old Sally had lived in the shanty near the sawmill since before most folks could remember. Some of the church ladies took her food now and then, but no one ever talked to her much except Violet. Old Sally told Violet about things like ghosts and haunts and spirits, and all about the three men. And then Violet told Guy.

That was when Guy stopped going to the outhouse for a while. Actually, he hadn't much liked going out there after dark, even before he heard about the three men. Like when Violet told him about the Paulsons' dead baby that Old Sally heard crying in the cemetery, and another time about how her cat wouldn't go in the back room of her cabin because somebody had died there. But after he heard about the three men there was a spell when he just couldn't go out into the dark anymore, past the woodshed with its open door and the shadowy rows of the berry patch. So on dark nights he peed near the back door—until Aunt caught him doing it.

Aunt got out the razor strop right away that time, but then Uncle Joe slowed things down by asking why Guy had been peeing in the ash pile. As soon as he could stop crying enough to talk, Guy told them what Violet had said about the three men, and Uncle Joe said that was enough to make anybody pee in the ash pile. Uncle Joe was like that. Sometimes Guy wished that Uncle Joe was really his uncle except that would make Aunt really his aunt. And the truth was, neither of them was kin at all. Guy just had to pretend they were because of what Aunt told Mrs.

Austin at the orphanage. Aunt said she'd come looking for her nephew and she'd found what she was looking for, but part of that wasn't true. The true part was that she found what she was looking for—someone big enough to do a man's work and small enough to be kept in line with a razor strop.

Usually Aunt was as quick with that old strop as Jesse James with a six-shooter, but that time it took her more than half an hour to get around to it. After Guy had told her and Uncle Joe what Violet had said, Aunt just stood there swishing the strop around like a flat blacksnake while she finished the argument with Uncle Joe.

It took a long time even though Uncle Joe didn't get to say very much, as usual. What he did get said was that he'd always thought it was too bad what happened to those three men, and he'd thought so at the time but he'd been too young to do much about it. But Aunt said that was just like him, sticking up for three foreigners against his own kith and kin. And even if they hadn't been the ones who stole the horses, like it turned out, they'd been up to no good, hanging around the valley like that, watching what folks were doing and trying to talk to people they had no business talking to. And the cabin catching fire the way it did when her pa and the rest of the men tried to smoke them out just saved the expense of a trial and three hanging ropes. The argument went on for a long time, but it wasn't long enough to make Aunt forget about what Guy had done—or about using the razor strop. Afterward Guy wondered if she might have forgotten if he'd told her everything Violet had said about the three men.

Up in the pepper tree it all came back sharp and clear, the way Violet had told it. He had time to think about all of it while the three men were still coming down the hill. It wasn't that they were moving so slowly. Their arms and legs swung back and forth so fast their raggedy gray tatters streamed out behind, and from beneath their feet dust whirled back in a twisting white cloud like smoke from a chimney. But they walked and walked and walked, and moved only from one fencepost to the next, as if they were walking forward and at the same time drifting backward on the east wind, like a swimmer going upstream. From behind a shivering fringe of pepper-tree leaves, Guy watched them coming and thought about what Violet had said.

"Old Sally told me they always come out when it's hot and dry with a Santa Ana blowing, the way it did the night it happened. On a hot, dry day they come up out of Grandpa Jackson's grave and start looking."

"What the Sam Hill are they doing in Grandpa Jackson's grave?" Guy had asked.

"That's where the men put them," Violet said, "because it was handy. Old Sally says that Grandpa Jackson was such a suspicious old coot that he made his kin dig his grave ahead of time so he could be sure they didn't skimp on it. So after the fire, there it was all ready, and that's where they put them. But now and then they come out again and go looking for the ones who did it."

"What would they do if they found any of them?" Guy asked.

"They already have," Violet said, nodding her head very slowly. "They've found them, all right. Some of them."

Guy swallowed hard. "Who—who'd they find?"

"Haven't you ever heard about Frank Appleby?"

"Mr. Appleby's name is Sam," Guy said.

Violet nodded. "Frank was his uncle. He was there that night when the cabin caught fire, and a few years after that his mare threw him one night down by the barranca. She was a lazy old thing he'd been riding for years, and Frank was a real good rider. But he'd a broken neck when they found him."

Guy felt his throat tighten like it did when Aunt got out the razor strop. He didn't like to think about Frank Appleby, or anybody, being alone at night in the wide dry riverbed, with its clumps of willow trees and big, dark boulders. Besides, he was pretty sure that Violet was just fibbing again.

"And then there was your aunt's pa. They got him, too," Violet said.

Guy had stared at her until his eyes began to feel dry and bulgy, but then he remembered something. "Nobody got Aunt's pa," he said, grinning with relief. "Aunt says her pa died right there in her house—of pneumonia. I remember her saying it lots of times."

Violet narrowed her eyes and tipped her secret smile into a knowing grin. "Maybe," she said. "And maybe not. Didn't she say how sudden it was? How everybody thought he just had a bad cold and how everybody thought—"

"That he was going to be up and about in a day or two," Guy finished for her, remembering Aunt's exact words. "And then the family all went off to the church picnic, and they stayed late because the weather was so fine and warm, and when they got back—"

Violet nodded. "And when they got back it was too late. And then there was Marybelle Mayberry."

"Marybelle who?" Guy had asked.

"Mayberry. The Mayberrys don't live here anymore. They moved away right after Marybelle disappeared."

"She disappeared?" Guy didn't like to think about disappearing. Just hearing the word made the scalp pucker all the way up the back of his head. Maybe it was because he'd always had a suspicion that there was a kind of belongingness that held people in place and without it there wasn't much to keep you from just waking up one morning and finding out you weren't there. There'd never been a whole lot for Guy to hold on to—not in the orphanage, and not much more in a house that belonged to people who were only pretend kin. And it was knowing that there'd be even less to hang on to when he was all alone and out on the open road that had kept him at Aunt's for so long, in spite of the razor strop. Disappearing was one thing he surely didn't like to hear about.

"Why'd they want to bother Marybelle?" he asked Violet. "There weren't any women at the cabin that night, were there?"

"Not that night. But Marybelle was the reason it happened. One of the reasons anyway. It was two girls who found out that the men were living in the old prospectors' cabin, and the two of them went around telling people about it. And that wasn't all they said."

"What else did they say?" Guy asked. He had a feeling he didn't want to hear any more about it, but he could tell that Violet wanted him to ask, so he did.

Violet rolled her eyes. "Those two girls said they were berrying along the creek bed and when they passed the cabin the men came out and called to them and asked them to come in."

Guy felt uneasy. He'd heard enough talk in the orphanage, the big boys mostly, whispering together out by the back fence, to have an idea why three strange men might ask some girls into their cabin. He had an idea, but he asked anyway. Looking down at his toe poking out through the hole in his left shoe, he asked, "Why'd they do that?"

Violet leaned forward. " 'Marybelle! Birdie!' is what those men called. 'Come in and have a cup of coffee,' and maybe they went in and maybe they didn't, but then they ran away and told their fathers; but Old Sally says, 'How'd those men know their names if those girls hadn't talked to them before, and maybe been there before and—' "

"Birdie!" Guy said, all of a sudden. "Not Birdie—"

Violet nodded. "*Aunt* Birdie," she said.

Guy gasped. He'd almost forgotten that Aunt's given name was Birdie. Aunt hated her name, and she wouldn't let anybody call her by it, not even Uncle Joe. Guy had seen it written once or twice, but it had taken him a minute or two to remember the writing when Violet had told him how Marybelle and Birdie had been a part of what happened that night at the old prospectors' cabin.

So perhaps the three men had been to Aunt's place once before and perhaps they had reason to come back again, and that was why Guy had been afraid to go outdoors after dark for a while last winter. But when Aunt had caught him peeing in the ash pile he hadn't told her everything. He hadn't mentioned Marybelle or Birdie. He hadn't dared—and besides, he figured he didn't need to. Aunt already knew what Marybelle and Birdie had, or hadn't, done.

The sunset had faded from fire to ash by the time the three men reached the edge of the apricot orchard, and in the deepening shadows it was hard to tell just where they went in, or how. There they were one minute, striding in and out of shadows, and the next minute they were gone; as if the orchard trees had reached out for them and swallowed them up. But even though he couldn't see them anymore he knew they were coming closer and closer, and all he could do was hang on to the pepper tree with all his strength and try to swallow the sound of his thundering heart. And then it was dark.

The Santa Ana was still blowing, and beneath the pepper tree the darkness flowed and moaned. Guy could hear the wavering moan and the hissing whisper of the leaves and nothing more. No sound came from the house or from in front of it where Old Jacob was still waiting at the hitching rail. The blinding flow of darkness was unbroken except where, through a blur of shivering black leaves, three dim squares of light had begun to glow. Lamps had been lit in the kitchen and parlor and in Aunt's bedroom upstairs. Aunt was waiting there, alone, behind the glowing windows, and somewhere in the invisible orchard the three men were striding forward against the dark wind.

Guy loosened his hold on the prickly limb and began to move backward. He'd almost reached the trunk of the tree when a new and larger patch of light shot out across the yard toward the pepper tree. And then Aunt appeared, a black paper woman, long and thin against the lamplight, with a black paper razor strop dangling from her hand. She stood there for a moment, and then she went back in. Guy heard the squeak of door hinges and saw the rectangle of light narrow away to blackness, and then he put his face down again against the peppery bark and closed his eyes. He didn't open them or turn his head when he heard the hinges creak again, and then a third time, and then a fourth.

Aunt left that night for Pasadena. She must have packed her things and loaded them into the buggy in a hurry, in the dead of night. When Uncle Joe came home she was already gone and so was Old Jacob and the buggy, and the house was in an awful mess. As soon as Uncle Joe found Guy, still hiding in the pepper tree, he showed him how the front door had been left wide open so that the Santa Ana had gotten in and blown out the lamps and scattered papers and dead leaves and all the ashes from the fireplace from one end of the house to the other. They cleaned the whole house early the next morning, but it went on smelling of ashes for two or three days.

Guy liked living alone with Uncle Joe. The apricots did very well that year, and in the fall Uncle Joe bought another riding horse and taught Guy how to ride and rope so he'd be ready for when they'd saved up enough money to start their beef herd. And sometimes Violet came over and taught Guy how to cook things that Uncle Joe wasn't very good at. Uncle Joe still didn't talk very much, but what he did say Guy liked to listen to almost as much as he liked to listen to Violet.

They hardly ever talked about Aunt, but once Uncle Joe said he guessed it was the Gardners' barn raising that did it, and if he'd known that was all it would take he'd have built a barn for the Gardners a whole lot sooner, even if he'd had to do it all by himself.

Guy didn't say anything. He never mentioned the three men. And he especially never mentioned the ashes. He never told Uncle Joe or anybody that one of the chores he'd done that day while Aunt was in town was to clean every last sliver of ashes out of the fireplace.

ZILPHA KEATLEY SNYDER, a native of rural central California, is among America's most honored writers for young readers. "I grew up way out in the country," she explains. "My life might have been boring if it had not been for two very important things—animals and books." Now she provides books for others. As a result of novels such as *The Egypt Game* (1966), *The Changeling* (1970), *The Headless Cupid* (1971), *The Witches of Worm* (1973), and *The Famous Stanley Kidnapping Case* (1978), among many others, she has garnered a list of honors that could fill this page.

"He reached up to touch his face. It was numb, and he realized he had been slapped. Pete raised his eyes to his mother's and knew that if he said one word, another slap was ready for him."

BASQUE HOTEL

ROBERT LAXALT

Summer

1

Along the length of Main Street, the business people of Carson City had come out to sweep the sidewalks in front of their shops and stores and little hotels. They did this when the sun had barely cleared the desert mountains to the east with a blinding burst of light, and before it had time to bake the sidewalks to a furnace heat.

The boy Pete had made the mistake of waking up before his brothers and sisters, and so his mother had thrust a broom into his hands. His father was usually the one who did the sweeping, but he had been gone all the night before on a mysterious errand. It was his coming home in the darkness before dawn that roused the boy, and he had gone outside in time to see the eastern horizon lined with an irregular band of red. To the west where the forested mountains reared, the sky was purple, so that the dying moon with one star at its tip still shone brilliantly white.

Pete told himself he had made a mistake in waking too early. But the truth was that he liked the sweeping and loved the morning. He liked particularly to sweep the cracks in the sidewalk, turning the broom on edge to clear the dust that had lodged there from the day before. He swept the cigar butts and the rare cigarette butts that the dandies smoked into the gutter, too, but only to make it worthwhile for the street cleaner who would come by later with his push broom and oversized dust pan and the metal trash can he pushed along on wheels.

The boy was lulled by the stillness of the early morning. Whenever he paused in his sweeping, there was no sound to be heard for minutes at a time. He did not count the crow of a late-waking cock from the edge of town or the chirping of birds in the cottonwoods and poplars that covered the back streets and the big white frame houses like a canopy. Those were sounds that were always there, so he did not even hear them.

A block away down the street, he saw the first squaws in their hooded blankets shuffle into sight and sit down on the sidewalk against the buildings to warm their old bones in the beginning sunlight. A block further on, he heard Frank the barber say good morning to one of the politicians who had come for his daily shave. Out of the corner of his eye, the boy saw a movement above him in one of the two windows that flanked the faded black lettering that said "The Basque Hotel," and he knew that Tristant the sheepherder was up and about. Then he heard the cough and sputter of an automobile being cranked to a start somewhere far down the street.

He began to sweep furiously to finish the sidewalk, taking care to go one width of a broom over the property line to the Columbo Hotel next door, because his father had told him that this was good manners to a neighbor. Piumbo, the fat proprietor of the Columbo, came outside just then with a broom. He was smoking a vile cigar that fouled the morning air, and his eyes were puffy and shot with red. The boy guessed this was from drinking too much wine, because he had heard snatches of Piumbo's singing far into the night. Piumbo acknowledged the gesture of the sweeping with a burst of mixed Italian and English, none of which the boy understood.

The time of stillness was gone, and the day had begun.

2

Pete was never sure whether Tristant the Basque sheepherder liked him
or not. It seemed to depend upon what time of day Tristant saw the boy.
This morning was one of those times when Tristant did not like him.
Pete understood why. The household was still asleep—except of course
for his mother, who always seemed to be awake. Tristant was sitting
alone at the long table that ran the length of the dining room. The box
of Kellogg's Corn Flakes was planted squarely in front of his place, and
he was shoveling cereal and milk into his mouth as fast as he could.
When Pete sat down, Tristant glanced at him venomously and moved
the box even closer to his bowl.

Pete could have started the day out well for Tristant if he had chosen
to. He knew and Tristant knew that the box of corn flakes was the only
one left in the hotel. Tristant's craving exceeded his own, because as
his father had told him, cereal and milk were something sheepherders
could not get in the hills.

Pete had already decided he did not want corn flakes this morning,
but coffee and milk with bread soaked in it instead. He also decided
to indulge the mean streak his mother said he possessed. From under
the fringes of his uncombed shock of brown hair, he peered around
the table as though making up his mind what he was going to have for
breakfast. From time to time, he glanced covertly at the box of corn
flakes. Tristant began to eat so fast he was dribbling milk from the corners of his mouth. When he emptied his bowl, he heaped it full again
with so much cereal that it was overflowing. Then he shook the box
and panic came into his eyes, because there was still some left.

Pete did not consider himself as mean as his mother made him out to
be. There was a point at which he relented a little. He did so now with
a sigh, as of deep sacrifice, and glumly filled his bowl with coffee and
milk and bread crusts and then poured a mound of sugar over it all.
Tristant stole a guilty look at the boy and slowed the pace of his eating

long enough to give him a smile that showed the gold teeth of which he was so proud. He mumbled good morning in Basque and the boy answered him in English.

3

After breakfast Pete went to the kitchen, but he did not stay long. It was uncomfortably hot from the fire in the massive black cooking range fed by firewood and would get more so through the day. Absently, he watched his mother chop vegetables on the cutting block with sure strokes of a big knife and drop them into the soup for the boarders' evening meal. Her forehead was beaded with sweat and her face was strained. Something was on her mind and she was in no mood for talking. Pete picked some flies off the hanging flypaper and went out into the back yard to feed MacTavish.

Shadowed by the big wooden hulk of the Columbo Hotel next door, the back yard was cool and quiet. The black earth had not begun to heat up yet, and next to the fence, it still held the night's dew. The boy felt peace wash over him again and he knew a twinge of remorse for having tormented poor Tristant, who was so ignorant he could barely speak English. He resolved not to fight with Tristant over the salad at supper that night, because that was supposed to be something else that sheepherders could not get in the hills.

The boy's sense of peace began to slip away when he saw Conchita stick her beak around the corner of the shed. Conchita belonged to the Columbo Hotel, but every once in a while she would flap her way over the high wooden fence to peck for worms where the ground stayed moist longer. She was wary because she expected to have a rock thrown at her. Pete did not disappoint Conchita. He threw the rock, but she ducked behind the shed just in time. Pete forgot her for the moment and went to the nail where he had tied the end of MacTavish's string.

MacTavish was a horny toad that Pete had found in the sagebrush outside the city limits. Pete had been afraid of MacTavish at first because he looked so ferocious with his horny covering, and had picked him up only on a dare. But MacTavish proved to be harmless and langorous, especially when his soft underbelly was scratched. In those moments, he would stretch out his legs and lie blissfully in Pete's palm.

Putting the flies into his shirt pocket, Pete sat down on the ground and began to pull in MacTavish's string. But only the slack came before he felt a tug on the other end of the string. The tug told Pete that something was wrong. MacTavish was too tiny to resist any kind of pull.

"I'll bet he went and got himself stuck behind the shed," Pete told himself. He got to his feet and went down the length of the string gently so as not to hurt MacTavish. He reached the shed and turned the corner.

At first, Pete could not believe what he was seeing. He closed his eyes and held them shut. When he opened them again, he knew his eyes had not deceived him. The end of the string led to Conchita's mouth and then disappeared. Nausea gripped Pete with an icy chill and his breakfast coffee was bitter in his mouth. Conchita cowered on the ground, but not from guilt. She was trapped like a fish on a hook.

Afterwards, Pete could not remember going berserk. The only things he remembered clearly were the chopping block and the feel of a hatchet in his hand. The rest of it came back in elusive snatches, Conchita snapping the string in her terror, the sound of flapping wings as she dodged the slashing blows, and Conchita clawing her way to the top of the fence.

Conchita must have been squawking and he must have been screaming, because his mother had burst out the door in her big white apron and was running toward him. She reached him as he was clambering over the fence in pursuit of Conchita. He felt the strong hands pinion his arms and set him down on the ground.

"What are you doing? Have you gone crazy?"

"God damn you! Leave me alone!"

And then lights exploded in his head. He reached up to touch his face. It was numb, and he realized he had been slapped. Pete raised his eyes to his mother's and knew that if he said one word, another slap was ready for him. The madness had dissipated and now his courage deserted him. He wilted and bowed his head and tasted injustice. She had not even bothered to ask why he had wanted to kill Conchita.

4

His brothers and sisters had been routed from the bedroom behind the kitchen and told to have their breakfast and go outside, so that Pete would be alone in his place of punishment. Sensing from their mother's expression that this time Pete had outdone himself, they dressed and left the room without saying a word to him. Only his baby sister, Michelle, had dared to look back once with tears in her eyes, and for that she received a spank on her bottom. Then his father had walked through on his way to shave. He must have heard what had happened, because he stared down at Pete from a great height with murder in his eyes. It was a look that Pete did not see often, but when he did, he felt the blood draining from his face and shivers course along his spine.

Because it would show if his father accosted him on the way back, Pete did not dare to begin plotting revenge. He waited until the sounds of the razor slapping against the strop, the scraping off of whiskers, and the hard pulling of the comb through iron black hair were done, and he hung his head while his father passed through again.

When he heard his father's muffled voice in the kitchen beyond, Pete went into his parents' bedroom. He knew exactly what he was going to do. On the dresser in the nearly bare room there was a metal box in which his mother kept the things that were private to her. Pete had come upon it one day by accident, not knowing what it was or what it contained. He had flipped open the top and seen that it was filled with such things as locks of baby hair tied with ribbons, letters written in a language he could not read, but which he supposed was Basque, and pictures of people he did not recognize. There was one picture, however, that seemed vaguely familiar to him.

It was of a young woman, almost a girl, leaning upon a pedestal. The arm that leaned on the pedestal was slender, and the hand that cupped the chin was fragile and white. The girl was more beautiful than anyone he had ever seen. She had a delicate face framed with soft black hair that was pulled upwards and kept in place by combs. But it was the eyes that held him most. They were huge and dark and wistful, and they concealed something that escaped him.

He had been about to put the picture back when he realized with happy surprise at first, and then with shock, that it was of his mother. He could not reconcile the girl in the picture with what his mother had become. The fragile hands had thickened and the slender arm was now grooved and muscled like a man's. Something of the delicate face remained, but the dark, wistful eyes were stern and hardened now.

Pete realized from that moment that he loved his mother. It was a secret he had never revealed by so much as a glance. It was a secret so guarded that he had never kissed his mother from that day on. And now, the revenge he had chosen was to destroy the picture.

Pete tiptoed past the iron bed to the dresser. Without remorse, he opened the box. His fingers knew exactly where the picture was, because he had last put it there himself. He jerked it out roughly and was about to tear it in two when the expression in the huge dark eyes caught him.

With stunning clarity, he saw what he had tried without success to see before. The eyes that looked out at him concealed a hurt so terrible that he felt his heart rip. Blinded by tears, he stuffed the picture back into the box and closed the lid.

Muted by distance, he heard the screen door to the kitchen slam shut and his sister Michelle's voice piping, "Mama! Mama! MacTavish is gone! I bet Conchita ate him."

You should have told me, his mother's eyes said when she came into the bedroom. *I would have understood.*

Pete wanted to tell her that she should have understood without words why he had gone crazy. She was his mother and by reason of that was supposed to know everything that went on in his mind. Then it came to him that this was not so, that there were things she could not know unless he told her. The knowledge opened up huge possibilities for secrecy in his life, but he was not sure he wanted that. The price of a secret, it seemed to him, was loneliness.

ROBERT LAXALT grew up in Carson City, Nevada. He has won major writing awards in both the United States and Spain for his novels exploring his Basque heritage. Laxalt has also been a correspondent for United Press, a Fulbright Scholar, and Writer-in-Residence at the University of Nevada, Reno. He is the author of eleven books of fiction and nonfiction.

"Cico reached into a clump of grass and brought out a long, thin salt cedar branch with a spear at the end. The razor-sharp steel glistened in the sun."

THE GOLDEN CARP

RUDOLFO ANAYA

"Hey Toni-eeeeee. Hulooooooo Antonioforous!"

A voice called.

At first I thought I was dreaming. I was fishing, and sitting on a rock; the sun beating on my back had made me sleepy. I had been thinking how Ultima's medicine had cured my uncle and how he was well and could work again. I had been thinking how the medicine of the doctors and of the priest had failed. In my mind I could not understand how the power of God could fail. But it had.

"Toni-eeeeee!" the voice called again.

I opened my eyes and peered into the green brush of the river. Silently, like a deer, the figure of Cico emerged. He was barefoot, he made no noise. He moved to the rock and squatted in front of me. I guess it was then that he decided to trust me with the secret of the golden carp.

"Cico?" I said. He nodded his dark, freckled face.

"Samuel told you about the golden carp," he said.

"Yes," I replied.

"Have you ever fished for carp?" he asked. "Here in the river, or anywhere?"

"No," I shook my head. I felt as if I was making a solemn oath.

"Do you want to see the golden carp?" he whispered.

"I have hoped to see him all summer," I said breathlessly.

"Do you believe the golden carp is a god?" he asked.

The commandment of the Lord said, Thou shalt have no other gods before me . . .

I could not lie. I knew he would find the lie in my eyes if I did. But maybe there were other gods? Why had the power of God failed to cure my uncle?

"I am a Catholic," I stuttered, "I can believe only in the God of the church—" I looked down. I was sorry because now he would not take me to see the golden carp. For a long time Cico did not speak.

"At least you are truthful, Tony," he said. He stood up. The quiet waters of the river washed gently southward. "We have never taken a nonbeliever to see him," he said solemnly.

"But I want to believe," I looked up and pleaded, "it's just that I have to believe in Him." I pointed across the river to where the cross of the church showed above the tree tops.

"Perhaps—" he mused for a long time. "Will you make an oath?" he asked.

"Yes," I answered. But the commandment said, Thou shalt not take the Lord's name in vain.

"Swear by the cross of the church that you will never hunt or kill a carp." He pointed to the cross. I had never sworn on the cross before. I knew that if you broke your oath it was the biggest sin a man could commit, because God was witness to the swearing on his name. But I would keep my promise! I would never break my oath!

"I swear," I said.

"Come!" Cico was off, wading across the river. I followed. I had waded across that river many times, but I never felt an urgency like today. I was excited about seeing the magical golden carp.

"The golden carp will be swimming down the creek today," Cico whispered. We scrambled up the bank and through the thick brush. We climbed the steep hill to the town and headed towards the school. I never came up this street to go to school and so the houses were not familiar to me. We paused at one place.

"Do you know who lives there?" Cico pointed at a green arbor. There was a fence with green vines on it, and many trees. Every house in town had trees but I had never seen a place so green. It was thick like some of the jungles I saw in the movies in town.

"No," I said. We drew closer and peered through the dense curtain of green that surrounded a small adobe hut.

"Narciso," Cico whispered.

Narciso had been on the bridge the night Lupito was murdered. He had tried to reason with the men, he had tried to save Lupito's life. He had been called a drunk.

"My father and my mother know him," I said. I could not take my eyes from the garden that surrounded the small house. Every kind of fruit and vegetable I knew seemed to grow in the garden, and there was even more abundance here than on my uncles' farms.

"I know," Cico said, "they are from the llano—"

"I have never seen such a place," I whispered. Even the air of the garden was sweet to smell.

"The garden of Narciso," Cico said with reverence, "is envied by all— Would you like to taste its fruits?"

"We can't," I said. It was a sin to take anything without permission.

"Narciso is my friend," Cico said. He reached through the green wall and a secret latch opened an ivy-laden door. We walked into the garden. Cico closed the door behind him and said, "Narciso is in jail. The sheriff found him drunk."

I was fascinated by the garden. I forgot about seeing the golden carp. The air was cool and clear, not dusty and hot like the street. Somewhere I heard the sound of gurgling water.

"Somewhere here there is a spring," Cico said, "I don't know where. That is what makes the garden so green. That and the magic of Narciso—"

I was bewildered by the garden. Everywhere I looked there were fruit-laden trees and rows and rows of vegetables. I knew the earth was fruitful because I had seen my uncles make it bear in abundance; but I never realized it could be like this! The ground was soft to walk on. The fragrance of sun-dazzling flowers was deep, and soft, and beautiful.

"The garden of Narciso," I whispered.

"Narciso is my friend," Cico intoned. He pulled some carrots from the soft, dark earth and we sat down to eat.

"I cannot," I said. It was silent and peaceful in the garden. I felt that someone was watching us.

"It is all right," Cico said.

And although I did not feel good about it, I ate the golden carrot. I had never eaten anything sweeter or juicier in my life.

"Why does Narciso drink?" I asked.

"To forget," Cico answered.

"Does he know about the golden carp?" I asked.

"The magic people all know about the coming day of the golden carp," Cico answered. His bright eyes twinkled. "Do you know how Narciso plants?" he asked.

"No," I answered. I had always thought farmers were sober men. I could not imagine a drunk man planting and reaping such fruits!

"By the light of the moon," Cico whispered.

"Like my uncles, the Lunas—"

"In the spring Narciso gets drunk," Cico continued. "He stays drunk until the bad blood of spring is washed away. Then the moon of planting comes over the elm trees and shines on the horde of last year's seeds— It is then that he gathers the seeds and plants. He dances as he plants, and he sings. He scatters the seeds by moonlight, and they fall and grow— The garden is like Narciso, it is drunk."

"My father knows Narciso," I said. The story Cico had told me was fascinating. It seemed that the more I knew about people the more I knew about the strange magic hidden in their hearts.

"In this town, everybody knows everybody," Cico said.

"Do you know everyone?" I asked.

"Uh-huh," he nodded.

"You know Jasón's Indian?"

"Yes."

"Do you know Ultima?" I asked.

"I know about her cure," he said. "It was good. Come on now, let's be on our way. The golden carp will be swimming soon—"

We slipped out of the coolness of the garden into the hot, dusty street. On the east side of the school building was a barren playground with a basketball goal. The gang was playing basketball in the hot sun.

"Does the gang know about the golden carp?" I asked as we approached the group.

"Only Samuel," Cico said, "only Samuel can be trusted."

"Why do you trust me?" I asked. He paused and looked at me.

"Because you are a fisherman," he said. "There are no rules on who we trust, Tony, there is just a feeling. The Indian told Samuel the story; Narciso told me; now we tell you. I have a feeling someone, maybe Ultima, would have told you. We all share—"

"Hey!" Ernie called, "you guys want to play?" They ran towards us.

"Nah," Cico said. He turned away. He did not face them.

"Hi, Tony," they greeted me.

"Hey, you guys headed for Blue Lake? Let's go swimming," Florence suggested.

"It's too hot to play," Horse griped. He was dripping with sweat.

"Hey, Tony, is it true what they say? Is there a bruja at your house?" Ernie asked.

"¡A bruja!" "¡Chingada!" "¡A la veca!"

"No," I said simply.

"My father said she cursed someone and three days later that person changed into a frog—"

"Hey! Is that the old lady that goes to church with your family?" Bones shrieked.

"Let's go," Cico said.

"Knock it off, you guys, are we going to play or not?" Red pleaded. Ernie spun the basketball on his finger. He was standing close to me and grinning as the ball spun.

"Hey, Tony, can you make the ball disappear?" He laughed. The others laughed too.

"Hey, Tony, do some magic!" Horse threw a hold around my neck and locked me into his half nelson.

"Yeah!" Ernie shouted in my face. I did not know why he hated me.

"Leave him alone, Horse," Red said.

"Stay out of it, Red," Ernie shouted. "You're a Protestant. You don't know about the brujas!"

"They turn to owls and fly at night," Abel shouted.

"You have to kill them with a bullet marked with a cross," Lloyd added. "It's the law."

"Do magic," Horse grunted in my ear. His half nelson was tight now. My stomach felt sick.

"Voodoo!" Ernie spun the ball in my face.

"Okay!" I cried. It must have scared Horse because he let loose and jumped back. They were all still, watching me.

The heat and what I had heard made me sick. I bent over, retched and vomited. The yellow froth and juice of the carrots splattered at their feet.

"Jesuschriss!" "¡Chingada!" "¡Puta!" "¡A la madre!"

"Come on," Cico said. We took advantage of their surprise and ran. We were over the hill, past the last few houses, and at Blue Lake before they recovered from the astonishment I saw in their faces. We stopped to rest and laugh.

"That was great, Tony," Cico gasped, "that really put Ernie in his place—"

"Yeah," I nodded. I felt better after vomiting and running. I felt better about taking the carrots, but I did not feel good about what they had said about Ultima.

"Why are they like that?" I asked Cico. We skirted Blue Lake and worked our way through the tall, golden grass to the creek.

"I don't know," Cico answered, "except that people, grown-ups and kids, seem to want to hurt each other—and it's worse when they're in a group."

We walked on in silence. I had never been this far before so the land interested me. I knew that the waters of El Rito flowed from springs in the dark hills. I knew that those hills cradled the mysterious Hidden Lakes, but I had never been there. The creek flowed around the town, crossed beneath the bridge to El Puerto, then turned towards the river. There was a small reservoir there, and where the water emptied into the river the watercress grew thick and green. Ultima and I had visited the place in search of roots and herbs.

The water of El Rito was clear and clean. It was not muddy like the water of the river. We followed the footpath along the creek until we came to a thicket of brush and trees. The trail skirted around the bosque.

Cico paused and looked around. He pretended to be removing a splinter from his foot, but he was cautiously scanning the trail and the grass around us. I was sure we were alone; the last people we had seen were the swimmers at the Blue Lake a few miles back. Cico pointed to the path.

"The fishermen follow the trail around the brush," he whispered. "They hit the creek again just below the pond that's hidden in here." He squirmed into the thicket on hands and knees, and I followed. After a while we could stand up again and follow the creek to a place where an old beaver dam made a large pond.

It was a beautiful spot. The pond was dark and clear, and the water trickled and gurgled over the top of the dam. There was plenty of grass along the bank, and on all sides the tall brush and trees rose to shut off the world.

Cico pointed. "The golden carp will come through there." The cool waters of the creek came out of a dark, shadowy grotto of overhanging thicket, then flowed about thirty feet before they entered the large pond. Cico reached into a clump of grass and brought out a long, thin salt cedar branch with a spear at the end. The razor-sharp steel glistened in the sun. The other end of the spear had a nylon cord attached to it for retrieving.

"I fish for the black bass of the pond," Cico said. He took a position on a high clump of grass at the edge of the bank and motioned for me to sit by the bank, but away from him.

"How can you see him?" I asked. The waters of the pool were clear and pure, but dark from their depth and shadows of the surrounding brush. The sun was crystalline white in the clear, blue sky, but still there was the darkness of shadows in this sacred spot.

"The golden carp will scare him up," Cico whispered. "The black bass thinks he can be king of the fish, but all he wants is to eat them. The black bass is a killer. But the real king is the golden carp, Tony. He does not eat his own kind—"

Cico's eyes remained glued on the dark waters. His body was motionless, like a spring awaiting release. We had been whispering since we arrived at the pond, why I didn't know, except that it was just one of those places where one can communicate only in whispers, like church.

We sat for a long time, waiting for the golden carp. It was very pleasant to sit in the warm sunshine and watch the pure waters drift by. The drone of the summer insects and grasshoppers made me sleepy. The lush green of the grass was cool, and beneath the grass was the dark earth, patient, waiting . . .

To the northeast two hawks circled endlessly in the clear sky. There must be something dead on the road to Tucumcari, I thought.

Then the golden carp came. Cico pointed and I turned to where the stream came out of the dark grotto of overhanging tree branches. At first I thought I must be dreaming. I had expected to see a carp the size of a river carp, perhaps a little bigger and slightly orange instead of brown. I rubbed my eyes and watched in astonishment.

"Behold the golden carp, Lord of the waters—" I turned and saw Cico standing, his spear held across his chest as if in acknowledgment of the presence of a ruler.

The huge, beautiful form glided through the blue waters. I could not believe its size. It was bigger than me! And bright orange! The sunlight glistened off its golden scales. He glided down the creek with a couple of smaller carp following, but they were like minnows compared to him.

"The golden carp," I whispered in awe. I could not have been more entranced if I had seen the Virgin, or God Himself. The golden carp had seen me. It made a wide sweep, its back making ripples in the dark water. I could have reached out into the water and touched the holy fish!

"He knows you are a friend," Cico whispered.

Then the golden carp swam by Cico and disappeared into the darkness of the pond. I felt my body trembling as I saw the bright golden form disappear. I knew I had witnessed a miraculous thing, the appearance of a pagan god, a thing as miraculous as the curing of my uncle Lucas. And, I thought, the power of God failed where Ultima's power worked; and then a sudden illumination of beauty and understanding flashed through my mind. This is what I had expected God to do at my first holy communion! If God was witness to my beholding of the golden carp, then I had sinned! I clasped my hands and was about to pray to the heavens when the waters of the pond exploded.

I turned in time to see Cico hurl his spear at the monstrous black bass that had broken the surface of the waters. The evil mouth of the black bass was open and red. Its eyes were glazed with hate as it hung in the air surrounded by churning water and a million diamond droplets. The spear whistled through the air, but the aim was low. The huge tail swished and contemptuously flipped it aside. Then the black form dropped into the foaming waters.

"Missed," Cico groaned. He retrieved his line slowly.

I nodded my head. "I can't believe what I have seen," I heard myself say. "Are all the fish that big here—"

"No," Cico smiled. "They catch two and three pounders below the beaver dam. The black bass must weigh close to twenty—" He threw his spear and line behind the clump of grass and came to sit by me. "Come on, let's put our feet in the water. The golden carp will be returning—"

"Are you sorry you missed?" I asked as we slid our feet into the cool water.

"No," Cico said, "it's just a game."

The orange of the golden carp appeared at the edge of the pond. As he came out of the darkness of the pond the sun caught his shiny scales and the light reflected orange and yellow and red. He swam very close to our feet. His body was round and smooth in the clear water. We watched in silence at the beauty and grandeur of the great fish. Out of the corners of my eyes I saw Cico hold his hand to his breast as the golden carp glided by. Then with a switch of his powerful tail the golden carp disappeared into the shadowy water under the thicket.

I shook my head. "What will happen to the golden carp?"

"What do you mean?" Cico asked.

"There are many men who fish here—"

Cico smiled. "They can't see him, Tony, they can't see him. I know every man from Guadalupe who fishes, and there ain't a one who has ever mentioned seeing the golden carp. So I guess the grown-ups can't see him—"

"The Indian, Narciso, Ultima—"

"They're different, Tony. Like Samuel, and me, and you—"

"I see," I said. I did not know what the difference was, but I did feel a strange brotherhood with Cico. We shared a secret that would always bind us.

RUDOLFO ANAYA is a native of rural New Mexico, which is the setting for "The Golden Carp," an excerpt from his famous novel *Bless Me, Ultima* (1972). In this segment, Tony encounters a mystical fish. That book is one of the few Chicano literary bestsellers. Among his other publications are *The Silence of the Llano: Short Stories* (1982), *The Legend of La Llorona* (1984), and *Lord of the Dawn: The Legend of Quetzalcoatl* (1987). Anaya is a unique writer who recognizes that "a storyteller tells stories for the community as well as for himself."

RURAL LIVES

"Either on the prairie or in town we were only a step from the wild, and we wavered between the pleasure it was to be part of it and the misguided conviction that it was in our interest to destroy it."

A FRONTIER BOYHOOD

WALLACE STEGNER

Eastend when we arrived was the Z-X ranch house and a boardinghouse for the crews building the grade for a Canadian Pacific branch line down from Swift Current. Its history, which none of us knew, was short and violent. Métis winterers had not ventured into the dark and bloody hills, disputed ground among the tribes, until 1867. In 1869 the Hudson's Bay Company built a post on Chimney Coulee, above the present town; it lasted one season before it was destroyed by the Blackfeet. In the 1870s the Mounties built a patrol post, first on Chimney Coulee, then on the river, to keep an eye on the Sioux and Nez Percés who had fled north of the line after the Indian wars. And in the 1880s cattle had begun coming in from Montana and had spread out over that noble range for twenty years. The terrible winter of 1906–07 put most of the outfits out of business. The Z-X was a remnant survivor, protected by its situation in the lap of the hills. Out of it our family and a dozen others carved a townsite.

Within a few weeks, when the rails were laid, the town grew by several derailed boxcars, old Pullmans, and a superannuated dining car. We lived the first winter in the dining car, considered pretty classy. Later we lived in a rented shack. After two years, my father built a house and a small barn down in the west end, on the river.*

The first year in Eastend was a chaos of experiences, good and bad. I caught lice from the half-Indian kids I played with and was fiercely shampooed with kerosene. I learned dirty words and dirty songs from the children of railroad construction workers and from Z-X cowpunchers. With other boys, I was induced to ride calves and lured into "shit fights" with wet cow manure in the Z-X corrals. Then or later I learned to dog-paddle, first in the irrigation ditch, later in the river, and I fished for suckers in the deep holes of the bends, and followed trails through willows that felt like authentic wilderness. Then or later we put .22 cartridges or blasting caps on the tracks ahead of approaching handcars or speeders, and once we got satisfactorily chased by the gandy dancers of the section crew. Around Christmas we all watched the first soldiers go off to the war, and then and afterward we had trouble with Canadian kids who said the United States was too yellow to get in the fight. They had a song for us:

> Here's to the American eagle
> He flies over mountain and ditch
> But we don't want the turd of your goddam bird
> You American son of a bitch

My brother, who was big for his age, and tough, fought every kid his size, and some bigger, in defense of America's honor. But we were ashamed, and we got an instructive taste of how it felt to be disliked for tribal affiliations that we hadn't really known we had.

The town grew around us, and incorporated us, and became our familiar territory: Main Street with its plank sidewalks, its drug and

---

*In the 1980s that house, now billed as one of the oldest houses in Saskatchewan, was bought by the local arts council under the leadership of Canadian writer Sharon Butala. Refurbished, repainted, and reroofed, it is being made into a refuge for writers who need a few months of total peace and quiet for finishing their books. I intend to haunt that house, just to keep track of what goes on.

grocery and hardware stores, its Pastime Theater, its lumberyard, its hotel and bank; Millionaire Row with its four or five bungalows with sweet peas and nasturtiums in their yards; Poverty Flat, where the two Chinese and some *métis* had shacks.

The people we knew were of many kinds: *métis*—French-Indian half-breeds—left over from the fur trade days; Texas and Montana cow-punchers left over from the cattle period; and a stew of new immigrants, Ontario men, cockneys fresh from another East End, Scandinavians moving up the migration route from the Dakotas to the Northwest, a few Jews, a Syrian family, a couple of Chinese, a Greek. Mark Twain, confronted by a colorful character, used to say, "I know him—knew him on the river." I could say, almost as legitimately, I know him—knew him in Eastend.

A young frontier gathers every sort of migrant, hope-chaser, rough-neck, trickster, incompetent, misfit, and failure. All kinds passed through our town, and some stayed, or were stuck. Our first doctor was a drifter and a drunk who finally died of eating canned heat. Our only dentist came through once a year, and in a week's stay did more harm than an ordinary dentist could have done in a decade. Our religious needs were served by two institutions: the shack-chapel and itinerant priest who took care of the *métis,* and the Presbyterian church with resident pastor who took care of everyone else. The Scandinavians, Ger-mans, Ontario men, Englishmen, and run-of-the-mill Americans, even the Syrian grocer and his family, became Presbyterians because that was where the principal social action was. The Jewish butcher, the cow-punchers, the two Chinese who ran the restaurant, and the Greek who took over from them—all without families—remained refractory and unassimilable.

When we arrived, and for a couple of years thereafter, the Frenchman River provided a habitat for beaver, muskrats, mink, weasels, sandhill cranes; in the willow breaks were big populations of cottontails and snowshoe hares preyed on by coyotes and lynxes. On the long, mainly roadless way to the homestead down on the Montana line—two days by lumber wagon with the cow tied behind, one day by buckboard (we called it a Democrat), seven or eight excruciating hours by Model T—we passed many sloughs swarming with nesting ducks. On the homestead itself, dry country far from any slough, it was all flickertails, prairie dogs, badgers, blackfooted ferrets, coyotes, gopher snakes, and hawks. That prairie, totally unsuited to be plowed up, was hawk heaven. I find now, decades later, when it has all been returned to grass, that ornithologists come from far-off universities to study ferruginous hawks there. I never knew their species name, but I knew their look in the sky or on a fencepost, and several times one fell out of the empty blue to strike a pullet within a few yards of me.

We plowed our first field, and dammed our coulee, and built our shack, in the summer of 1915, and thereafter we spent the summers on the homestead, the winters in town. It was an uneven division, for in that latitude a wheat crop, from seedtime to harvest, took only about three months. But either on the prairie or in town we were only a step from the wild, and we wavered between the pleasure it was to be part of it and the misguided conviction that it was in our interest to destroy it. There are two things that growing up on a belated western frontier gave me: an acquaintance with the wild and wild creatures, and a delayed guilt for my part in their destruction.

I was a sickly child, but hardly a tame one. Like all the boys I knew, I had a gun, and used it, from the age of eight or nine. We shot at anything that moved; we killed everything not domesticated or protected. In winter we trapped the small fur-bearers of the river bottom; in summer my brother and I spent hours of every day trapping, shooting, snaring, poisoning, or drowning out the gophers that gathered in our wheatfield and the dependable water of our "rezavoy." We poisoned out the prairie dogs, and incidentally did in the blackfooted ferrets that lived on them—ferrets that are now the rarest North American mammals. We didn't even know they were ferrets; we called them the big weasels. But we killed them as we killed everything else. Once I speared one with a pitchfork in the chickenhouse and was sickened by its ferocious vitality, dismayed by how hard the wild died. I had the same feeling when I caught a badger in a gopher trap. I would gladly enough have let him loose, but he was too fierce, and lunged at me too savagely, and in the end I had to stone him to death.

Nobody could have been more brainlessly and immorally destructive. And yet there was love there, too. We took delight in knowing intimately the same animals we killed. Our pets were all captives from the wild—burrowing owls, magpies, a coyote pup, a ferret that I caught in a gopher trap and kept in a screened beer case and fed with live gophers. One of the first short stories I ever wrote, "Bugle Song," was a moment from that tranced, murderous summer season when I went from poetry and daydreaming to killing, and back to daydreaming. "Bugle Song" is an idyll counterweighted by death.

Our neighbors were few, and miles away, most of them across the line in Montana. For two weeks at a time we might see no one but ourselves; and when our isolation was broken, it was generally broken by a lonesome Swedish homesteader who came over ostensibly to buy eggs, but more probably to hear the sound of a human voice. We welcomed him. We were as hungry for the sound of a human voice as he was.

I am somewhat skeptical of the fabled western self-reliance, because as I knew it, the West was a place where one depended on neighbors and had to give as well as get. In any trouble while we were on the homestead, I ran, or rode one of the horses, four or five miles to get Tom Larson or Ole Telepo or someone else to help. They came to us the same way. And yet there is *something* to the notion of western independence; there is something about living in big empty space, where people are few and distant, under a great sky that is alternately serene and furious, exposed to sun from four in the morning till nine at night, and to a wind that never seems to rest—there is something about exposure to that big country that not only tells an individual how small he is, but steadily tells him *who* he is. I have never understood identity problems. Any time when I lay awake at night and heard the wind in the screens and saw the moon ride up the sky, or sat reading in the shade of the shack and heard the wind moan and mourn around the corners, or slept out under the wagon and felt it searching among the spokes of the wheels, I knew well enough who, or *what*, I was, even if I didn't matter. As surely as any pullet in the yard, I was a target, and I had better respect what had me in its sights.

I never came out to the homestead in June without anticipation and delight. I never returned to town in early September without a surge of joy—back to safety and shelter, back to the river and the willow breaks, back to friends, games, Sunday school parties, back to school, where I could shine.

It is a common notion that children reared in lonely, isolated places yearn for the color and action and excitement and stimulation of gaudier places. Adolescents, maybe; not children of the age I was, in the place where I lived. Everything I knew was right around me, and it was enough.

WALLACE STEGNER, dean of writers in the American West, was born in 1909 in Iowa, raised in Saskatchewan, Montana, and Utah, and lived for fifty years in California. Among his rich output were the novel *Angle of Repose,* which won 1972's Pulitzer Prize; a biography of Bernard DeVoto, *The Uneasy Chair,* which won the National Book Award for nonfiction in 1974; and another novel, *The Spectator Bird,* winner of the National Book Award for fiction in 1977. He died following an automobile accident in 1993 as this book was being prepared. "A Frontier Boyhood" is excerpted from "Finding a Place: A Migrant Childhood," an essay that appears in *Where the Bluebird Sings to the Lemonade Springs* (1992).

"The mare ambled around a corner into Mill Street, pausing obediently at one gate or another while the boy rolled a paper and crammed it between the pickets. It was time to make up his mind which daydream he was going to entertain himself with."

THE NEWSBOY

LEVI PETERSON

Albert was the town newsboy—a small, sweet-faced, knobby-jointed kid of eleven. One August day he came out of the house wearing a baseball cap and a *Deseret News* T-shirt. He bridled an old mare and shoved a saddle onto her back. As he cinched up, the mare tried to bite him and he gave her a punch in the nose. He threw his paperbag over the cantle, stood on an upside-down grain bucket, and climbed aboard. He pulled his belt from the loops of his pants and slapped the mare on the flank. She groaned and ambled into the street.

Down the road roared an open Model A spewing gravel and stirring dust. In it were Ralph Drayton and his rowdy friends, none old enough to have a driver's license. As they careened by, one of them shouted an obscenity at Albert. He shook a fist and they laughed and shouted more dirty words.

Albert tied the mare at the back of the grocery store on Main Street and carried the paperbag around front. A bus from Salt Lake had dropped off a big bundle of the *Deseret News* and a small bundle of the *Salt Lake Tribune*.

Only backsliders and gentiles subscribed to the *Tribune*. Albert knelt, clipped the wires, and counted both bundles. Exactly the expected number. The headlines said the Japanese had surrendered.

Cull Stevens, owner of the store, came out carrying a scoop shovel. The boy said, "Look here. The war's over."

"Everybody knows that," Cull said. "It's been on the radio all day."

"Nobody told me."

"Your dad ought to buy a radio that works," Cull said. "Also, you never cleaned up where your horse dumped like I told you. Take this shovel and go clean up the mess."

Albert carried the shovel around back and scooped up the dried droppings beneath the mare and deposited them in a trash barrel. Luckily there was nothing fresh. When he had finished, he meandered through the store and paused in front of the candy counter. He was out of nickels. For a moment he felt like there wasn't much to live for. He went out and stuffed his papers into the double bag. Then he sat on the bag, opened a paper to the comics, and started to read.

Cull came out again and said, "It seems like you ought to get your papers delivered before midnight." The boy picked up his bulging bag and staggered around to the mare. Cull followed, saying, "Garth Hazelton got his paper while you were around back. I took mine too." The boy counted the papers again. Three short. No matter how many times he counted, he always came up with a different total. He slapped his forehead two or three times so that he would remember not to deliver extra papers to Cull and Garth.

The mare ambled around a corner into Mill Street, pausing obediently at one gate or another while the boy rolled a paper and crammed it between the pickets. It was time to make up his mind which daydream he was going to entertain himself with. Sometimes he was a Liberator pilot bombing Germany and sometimes a tank commander on Guadalcanal. Sometimes he was a cavalry officer fighting Indians and sometimes an outlaw who kidnapped Paula Ruckhart. Paula was a blond girl who had moved to town last spring. She had sat across the room from him at school and had never said hello.

He decided to kidnap Paula. At first petty distractions got in the way of his daydream. For example, Ben Campole was painting his eaves, and Aunt Mary Goldwin was boiling her clothes the old-fashioned way in a kettle under her elm trees. Before long Albert switched on the movie projector in his mind. He saw the outlaw tether his enormous black horse at the church gate. A hymn came from the open doors of the meetinghouse. When the outlaw entered, every person turned to look. The hymn died abruptly, mouths gaped, bodies froze. The churchgoers knew who he was because the outlaw had harried and pillaged the countryside for months. He stopped before the pew in which the Ruckhart family sat. "Oh, no," Mrs. Ruckhart gasped, "please, not our Paula." Mr. Ruckhart rose half up. The outlaw waved his rifle menacingly and Mr. Ruckhart sank feebly into his seat. Paula emerged from the pew. Her golden hair was fluffed into fine curls; she wore a filmy summer dress. Trembling and weeping, she looked back at her mother. Hardening his heart, the outlaw gave a jerk of his head and turned on his heel. She followed obediently. Outside he mounted the horse and pulled Paula up behind. Although no one inside stirred, he fired a warning shot in the air. The horse wheeled and with clattering hooves bore the outlaw and his clinging prize away through the streets, down a lane, and into the junipers and sage.

On Back Street a fight between Bant and Lois Soderquist interrupted his daydream. Their screen door flew open and Bant dashed out in his stocking feet. Lois chased close behind, waving a stick of firewood. She wore a denim skirt and Wellington boots. After they had circled the house twice, Bant scrambled up a ladder that leaned against the eaves and by sheer momentum went on up the steep roof to the chimney. With a whimper he threw his arms around the chimney and hugged it like a long-lost brother.

Lois walked to the gate. The boy rolled a *Tribune* and handed it to her. "The war's over," he said.

"Like hell it is," she said. "It ain't but begun." She picked up rocks and began chucking them at Bant.

"Goldang you!" Bant roared, easing himself around to the opposite side of the chimney.

She laughed and threw harder. "He's afraid of high places," she said to Albert. Finally she took the paper and went into the house.

The boy gave the mare a lick with his belt and started on. "Hold on there," Bant shouted from the chimney. "You haven't collected yet this month. Come up here and I'll give you a dollar and a quarter."

It was an offer Albert couldn't ignore because, two months out of three, Bant failed to pay. He tied the mare to the fence, went to the door, and stuck in his head. Lois was smoking a cigarette and reading the paper. There was dust on the window sills and eggshells on the floor. "Is it all right if I go up and collect off Bant?" the boy asked.

"Jeez, yes," she said, "take anything you can get off that skinflint."

He found the roof much steeper than it looked from the ground. When he arrived at the chimney, Bant made a grab for him and Albert tumbled half down the roof before the splintering shingles stopped him. "Come on up here, feller," Bant said, again clinging to the chimney with both arms. He was a lank old cowboy who spent weeks at a time on a ranch in Nevada. His face was seamed and covered by grizzled whiskers. "Come on up here," he repeated.

"Naw," the boy said, backing down to the ladder, "I've got to get my newspapers delivered." He could see Bant was so scared that he'd grab him the way a drowning man grabs a swimmer and then they'd both roll down the roof and fall off.

The boy positioned the mare in a ditch and climbed into the saddle. At the next house he got off, tied her again, and went to the door. Mrs. Hobson, a widow who had once been his schoolteacher, answered his knock. "The war's over," he said, spreading a *Deseret News* so she could see the headlines.

She took the paper and said, "Albert, that's very thoughtful of you to call the surrender to my attention even though it's been on the radio all day. Thank God our soldiers can come home now. I suppose, of course, you've heard that poor Walt Hampstead was killed last week in training at that California airfield. They've shipped his body home. The funeral will be tomorrow morning."

"No, ma'am, I didn't hear that from anybody," Albert said. "The reason I stopped is Bant Soderquist is on his roof and doesn't know how to get down."

"My goodness," Mrs. Hobson said, coming onto her porch and gazing where he pointed. Beyond her corral and chicken coops they could see Bant on his roof, still hugging the chimney.

"His wife chased him there," the boy went on. "He won't let loose of the chimney. He's afraid of high places."

"That new wife of Bant's! If she isn't a scandal!" Mrs. Hobson exclaimed. "Well, come in and we'll phone somebody to come get him down."

Mrs. Hobson's old father, Simon Summerill, sat in the living room with a blanket over his legs. She had brought him from Arizona to live out his dotage. Across one cheek he had a scar as wide as a finger, which he had got in a fight with Apaches. Mrs. Hobson shouted into Simon's ear, "Father, please tell Albert a pioneer story while I phone the fire department to come get Bant Soderquist off his roof." She spoke to Albert as she left the room. "Father was one of the pioneers. You ask him to tell you a story. Get right up close and talk into his left ear."

Before Albert could say a word, old Simon began to speak, his big Adam's apple working up and down like the pump on a shotgun. "My boy Samuel lives in Salt Lake. The story he tells is that there were some fellows digging a new grave with a bulldozer in the city cemetery and they knocked open a coffin in the next grave. There wasn't anything in the coffin except somebody's temple clothes, which were folded up nice and neat and laid in the bottom. There wasn't a body in the coffin. Just those temple clothes folded up nice and neat. Do you know what that means? It means the Resurrection is going on all the time. That body has been resurrected. You'd find hundreds of empty coffins if you'd dig up all the graves in that cemetery."

"Now, Father, tell him how you got your scar," said Mrs. Hobson, who had returned.

"That's okay," the boy said, "I've got to get on delivering my papers."

She followed him onto the porch, and both gazed again at Bant, still huddled in a tight embrace with his chimney. Just then the siren on top of the town hall began to wail, the signal for the members of the volunteer fire department to assemble.

"They'll get him down very shortly now," Mrs. Hobson said with satisfaction. "It was very civic-minded of you, Albert, to pause in your busy schedule and seek help for him."

Albert rode up Back Street, cramming papers between pickets or giving them a toss onto porches and flagstone walks. At one place the paper skidded into irrigation water that had ponded on a lawn, and Albert had to dismount and retrieve the soggy paper. He set a dry paper on the porch and gave the railing a kick because he'd have to carry the ruined paper home and his brothers and sisters would complain that they always had to take the rejects. About that time Ralph Drayton and his hellraising buddies came roaring and weaving down Back Street in their Model A. As the car raced by, they again shouted obscenities at Albert.

While he rode up Back Street and out Cemetery Lane, Albert resumed his daydream about kidnapping Paula Ruckhart. He imagined himself and Paula in a cave concealed by thick timber. The cavern was deep and spacious and carpeted with bearskin rugs so thick and furry a person could wander around barefooted. A warm, romantic fire flickered and flamed without the slightest breath of smoke. A problem had come up, which the outlaw calmly discussed with Paula. Supplies were low and he would have to ride out to pillage and plunder. The question was whether he would have to leave her tied up. She promised she wouldn't run away. Furthermore, she cried and wrung her hands and wondered why he couldn't take her with him. For days she had wept for her mother and father and brothers and sisters, but now she was weeping for him. He led her to her bed, tucked her under a bearskin, patted her head three or four times, and vowed to return safe and sound. Strapping on his ammunition belt, he turned for a last look and she pouted her sweet little lips and blew him a kiss.

Down the lane Albert tied the mare at Sawyers' gate and knocked at the house. Mrs. Sawyer told him her husband was in the cemetery digging a grave for Walt Hampstead. Albert crossed the cattleguard behind the house and threaded his way among the graves. Rabbit bush and tall yellow bunchgrass grew thick at the edge of the cemetery. Mr. Sawyer labored shoulder-deep in the fresh grave. He was pudgy and bald and heaved his pick with an awkward lurch. He had suffered a collapsed lung at Pearl Harbor and had been discharged from the navy, and the church had given him a job as janitor of the meetinghouse and sexton of the cemetery.

"The war's over," the boy said, spreading out a *Tribune*.

"Too bad," the man said. "Now the bottom will drop out of the black market."

"I've come by to collect. I missed you last week."

Mr. Sawyer grasped his shovel and began to throw out gravel. Albert peered into the pit. "Mrs. Hobson's dad says the Resurrection is going on all the time," he said. "Up in Salt Lake somebody was bulldozing in the graveyard and they knocked open a coffin. There wasn't a body in it. Just temple clothes folded up nice and neat. Maybe they ought to open up Walt Hampstead's coffin. Maybe he wouldn't be in it. Maybe he would already be resurrected."

"What about my dead lung?" Mr. Sawyer grunted. "I suppose that's already been resurrected." He pulled a little ladder into the grave and clambered out. He faced Albert. "Look up there," he commanded, pointing to the sky. "Do you see any angels? Look hard! Do you see any? Any at all?"

Albert peered into the silver blue sky. "Hell, no, you don't see any angels," Mr. Sawyer, said, setting off toward the house.

Inside, loaves of bread smoked on the counter, and three Sawyer girls sat at a table eating bread and honey. "Give this boy some of that hot bread while I see if I don't have some cash in my other pants," Mr. Sawyer said to his wife. Albert sat at the table and slathered a fat slice of bread with butter and honey. He took enormous bites and followed them with gulps of milk. He looked over the Sawyer girls to see if one of them resembled Morris Hancher, because Morris Hancher was the man Mrs. Sawyer had committed adultery with while Mr. Sawyer recuperated in a navy hospital in San Diego. Though Mrs. Sawyer had made a public confession of her sin, she had been excommunicated. The girls were thin and freckled and had pigtails. They didn't look like anybody but themselves.

Mr. Sawyer came from the bedroom and paid double so that Albert wouldn't have to waste his time trying to catch him next month. "You know why there wasn't a body in that coffin Simon Summerill told you about?" he asked the boy. "It wasn't because the Resurrection is going on all the time. It was because somebody stole the body and sold it to the university medical school. The Resurrection! My God!"

Mrs. Sawyer followed Albert from the house when he had finished eating. She wore a faded cotton dress and had a sad face. While the boy maneuvered his mare close to an anthill so he could mount, Mrs. Sawyer said, "Don't you let my husband put any bad ideas into your head. He isn't mean to me or anybody else, but he doesn't believe in anything. You mind your daddy and mamma and you listen to what your Sunday school teacher tells you."

"Yes, ma'am," the boy said, giving the mare a thwack. "Thanks for the bread and honey."

He emerged from the lane and delivered along Springer Street. The mare paced briskly because they were for the moment headed toward home, and the boy slipped into his daydream. He saw the outlaw enter the grocery store. The terrified cashier clapped her hands over her mouth. Cull Stevens came from behind the meat counter carrying a cleaver. The outlaw heaved a can of condensed milk, smashing a neon clock on the wall. Cull dropped the cleaver. Turning his back contemptuously, the outlaw picked out his booty: a bottle of red hair oil for himself, a purple lipstick for Paula, a box of canned soup, half a dozen cartons of candy bars, and a case of orange soda pop. He forced Cull to carry the plunder outside, roll it in a tarp, and lash it behind his saddle. The outlaw mounted, wheeled the horse about, and urged it back until its rump poised precisely before the door. There the animal obligingly did a mess. "Get a scoop and clean that up," the outlaw ordered, pointing at the stinking green pile. Then he spurred the horse lightly and cantered down the street. Mothers dashed from houses and caught up their children from lawns and sidewalks. Their worry was needless: the outlaw didn't hurt little kids.

Albert turned into Culver Street and heard a violin playing "The Last Rose of Summer." It was Osborne Wallerton, the town musician, practicing on his front porch. Wild bunchgrass and yucca grew on his lot instead of lawn, garden, and trees because he lived above the ditch and was too frugal to irrigate with community water. When he saw the boy and the mare, the musician tucked the violin under an arm and picked his way barefooted along the gravel path to the gate.

"The war's over," Albert said.

"A solemn hush falls upon the world," Osborne replied, taking his paper.

"They're bringing Walt Hampstead home. Mr. Sawyer is digging his grave."

"So I would expect. I'm rehearsing a few pieces for his funeral."

The mare extended her neck across the aging barbed wire fence and tried to crop a strand of bunchgrass. Osborne tapped her on the nose with the violin bow. As she retreated, he said, "From time to time your horse fouls my gateway."

The boy looked contrite. "She doesn't have any manners at all."

"It is the course of nature," Osborne went on. "In general the horse is a noble animal. The emperor Caligula appointed his favorite horse to be a priest, senator, and consul." Osborne scratched his heel with the point of the bow. "Poor Walt Hampstead," he mused. "He was gifted with the trombone. Now he is merely manure. But a divine manure! A vintage which the Lord hath trampled in his wrath." The mare made another pass at the bunchgrass, and he tapped her again on the nose. "Mmmm," he went on, "the music for the funeral should be grand and heroic. 'The Battle Hymn of the Republic' is exactly what we need." He thrust the paper into his waist and positioned the violin under his chin. He turned and picked his way along the path, playing the piece he had named.

Abruptly he turned about, calling to Albert, "You don't intend to be a truck driver when you grow up, do you?"

The confounded boy didn't answer.

"Make something of yourself," the musician commanded, turning and again drawing his bow across his instrument.

The boy turned into West Street. At the gate of Peach Robinson's corral stood a gaunt brindle cow with large moon eyes. She seemed thirsty. Peach Robinson was notorious for neglecting livestock. The next barnyard belonged to Harold Surrey, the government trapper. Harold's battered Ford pickup stood just inside the open gate, its radiator hissing, its door hanging open. Harold stood in the back, kicking coyote carcasses out the open tailgate and shouting at his big Airedale dogs, which trotted round and round, whining and barking. While the mare pricked her ears suspiciously, the boy gazed at the tawny bodies stacked like cordwood eight or ten deep. The coyotes had crushed skulls, Harold having caught them in steel traps and finished them with a blow from a hammer.

"The war's over," Albert said, unfolding a *Deseret News.*

"By golly!" said Harold, who had been in camp. He took the paper and read. "By gum, it really is! Well, I say hooray. We shouldn't be killing people, not even if they're sons of bitches like those Germans and Japanese. All that killing isn't natural."

"They're having Walt Hampstead's funeral in the morning," Albert said. "He got killed in an airplane crash in California."

"My gosh, is that true?" Harold said in astonishment. "I'm sorry to hear it. Now isn't that terrible, isn't that just the irony of fate? An airplane crash in California!" One of the coyote carcasses which Harold had kicked out was twitching. He got a hammer from the cab and gave the coyote another blow on the skull.

"Peach Robinson's cow looks thirsty," Albert said. "Do you think it'd be all right if I let her out to the ditch?"

"You bet," Harold said.

Albert tied the mare to a post and opened the gate. The gaunt cow paced across the street, her udder swaying, and thrust her muzzle into the brown water. When she had satisfied her thirst, Albert returned her to the corral and asked Harold for a leg-up into his saddle. Seated, he said, "Mrs. Hobson's dad says the Resurrection is going on all the time. Somebody was digging in the Salt Lake graveyard and they knocked open a coffin. They couldn't find a body in it. There were some temple clothes folded up nice and neat. That means the Resurrection is going on all the time."

"A lot of tumbleweeds blow through old Simon Summerill's head!" Harold exclaimed. "He thinks he can remember whether Noah's wife was blond or brunette."

At the next intersection Albert encountered Shirley Kelsey trailing a cow which without question had just paid a visit to Layton Johnson's bull. Astride a pinto pony, Shirley wore dirty jeans and runover cowboy boots. She was very pleased to have Albert's company, telling him, "Me and Dad drowned gophers today. You dig into their burrow with a shovel and clean the dirt out of the hole and you stick in the hose and turn it on. Sometimes the gophers make a dash for it and our dog gets them. It's keen!"

As they passed the movie house at the intersection of Center and Main, the midweek matinee adjourned, and a swarm of children and a few adults came blinking out into the late-afternoon sun. The cow walked among them, her back humped and her tail extended. The boy wished he was a gopher, not one that Shirley and her father had drowned, of course, but another gopher comfortably isolated in a dark tunnel. It was terrible how brazen cattle were about doing the dirty deed.

One day while Albert was eight Shirley had called him into a barn. 'Do you want to play buck and doe?" she asked.

"I've got to get home," he said.

"People make babies just like a ram and a ewe," she said.

"That's nothing new. I knew that a long time ago."

"Do you want to climb up in the loft with me?" she asked. "I'll let you look at me if you'll let me look at you."

Later, after they had buckled their belts and climbed down the ladder, she said, "Don't you tell anybody." She didn't need to worry. A person couldn't have pried his mouth open with a crowbar. For two or three months he couldn't say his evening prayers. Night after night, kneeling at his bedside under his mother's watchful eye, he silently counted to a hundred and said amen.

Saying good-bye to Shirley, Albert turned into Webster Street. For a minute or two he struggled to remember the lesson in Sunday school last week. The lesson might have been about Samson smiting the Philistines hip and thigh with a great slaughter or about Jesus resisting the temptation to turn stones into bread. The boy believed if he had paid closer attention to his teacher a certain rotten idea wouldn't now be roiling around inside his head like a carp in a muddy slough.

As he rode toward the cave with his booty, the outlaw had in mind that after supper he would ask Paula if she wanted to play buck and doe. Even if she didn't, he'd make her. There was no advantage in being an outlaw if he couldn't do immoral, outrageous things. When he arrived, Paula emerged and helped him unpack and carry in the stolen goods. She chattered cheerfully, obviously delighted by his safe return. He chopped wood, built up the fire, and prepared an elegant supper of macaroni and cheese and orange soda pop. He believed it a man's duty to do the cooking in camp. After supper he and Paula washed the dishes. Outside darkness had fallen; inside the fire glinted and gleamed. The outlaw felt awful. He didn't have the courage to tell Paula she had to take off her panties.

"When do I get to go home?" she asked.

"Aw, heck," the outlaw said, "you don't want to go home yet. We're just starting to have fun."

"I'm not having any fun," she said. "I'm getting bored. Sitting around this cave is worse than practicing piano all day."

"I'll tell you what," he said. "Tomorrow we'll climb into that big cottonwood in the hollow, and we'll wait until a couple of elk graze along underneath. Then we'll drop onto their backs and hang on tight to their antlers. You'll have the ride of your life."

"Gee," she said, "that'd be fun. We'll really do that?"

"You bet!"

"All right," Paula said, "I don't mind if I don't go home just yet."

Albert arrived at the gate of Ross McCrimmon, deputy sheriff. Ross pushed a mower across his lawn with his left arm because his right elbow was in a cast. His cousin Butch McCrimmon sat with legs dangling from the porch railing. Behind Butch stood Ross's wife.

"The war's over," Albert said, unfurling a *Deseret News*. Ross stepped close, tilted his head, and stared morosely at the headline through his bifocals. Then he gave the mower another shove.

"I wonder if they'll show us those atomic bombs blowing up them Jap cities in the newsreels," Butch said. "It's too bad the war's over. Pretty soon there won't be anything interesting in the newsreels except train wrecks and hotel fires."

Butch took off a shoe and shook out a pebble. "Isn't it the truth," he went on, "that Hitler and Tojo and Mussolini should have had better sense than to get the United States into the war. They should've known we'd whip them. It's football that makes America strong. You can't whip a nation that plays football. Our soldiers are too fast."

"It was factories that beat them," Mrs. McCrimmon said. "Factories and food, tanks and ships."

"It was high school athletics," Butch insisted. "Our boys dodge too fast. They don't make an easy target."

"You never shot at an American," the deputy said. "If you had, you might think different." Ross gazed again at Albert with a long, sad face, as if he considered it wicked to smile while there were so many un-punished lawbreakers in the world. His eyes were the kind that could peer through concrete slabs. He could probably tell what a kid had been daydreaming about five minutes ago. He'd know that the outlaw had kidnapped Paula Ruckhart and had robbed Cull Stevens's store.

Though Albert hated a tattletale, he had to do something to shift Ross's attention. "Ralph Drayton has been tearing around town in his dad's Model A," he blurted. "Him and his buddies are shouting vulgar things at people."

"That Drayton kid has just barely turned fifteen," Mrs. McCrimmon said. Mrs. McCrimmon kept a census of all the underage drivers in town. Also, if somebody broke into the high school shop and stole some wrenches, she knew whose shed ought to be searched.

She went into the house and came out with a black report book. Ross had begun to mow again in his slow, awkward way. "Are you just going to let that Drayton kid terrorize the town?" she asked.

"We'll go talk to his dad and mom tonight," Ross said.

At the east end of Webster Street, Albert tied the mare to a gate and went around to the back of a tall red brick house built in pioneer times. Minerva Elverson, the spinster who owned it, rented the front and the upstairs and lived in the back. The path along the side of the house was dark with overhanging lilacs and grapevines. The boy knocked, and without a sound Miss Elverson suddenly appeared in the screen door. Her spine was curved, her cheekbones angular, her eyes haggard.

"The war's over," Albert said.

"I'm grateful," she said, "though it often seemed I had only imagined there was a war."

"I've come to collect," he said.

She opened the door and motioned him in. Unwashed dishes cluttered the kitchen table; the odor of rancid butter hung in the air. He followed her into the dim living room. Beneath a glass dome reposed a bouquet of paper pansies. She gestured him toward the sofa and took the deep chair just opposite. She rummaged in her purse and handed him a dollar and a quarter. He stood and stuffed the money into his pocket.

"Would you like fifty cents extra?" she asked, deliberately laying out two quarters on the side table. "Would you let me hold you for a minute?" she said. He didn't understand. She picked through her purse again and pulled out a bill. "A dollar," she said, "if you will sit on my lap. Just for a moment."

He pursed his lips and shook his head. She said, "Your mother has eight to hold. I don't have any." He fingered the dollar. "I had a little brother who died," she said.

"Just for a minute," he replied at last, pocketing the dollar.

She pulled him into her lap and pressed his head against her chest. She pushed off his baseball cap and tangled her fingers in his hair. "My little one, my poor lost little one," she wept.

"I'm not lost," he insisted.

As he slid off her lap and put on his cap, she gave him the quarters as a bonus. "Please don't tell anybody," she pleaded.

"No, ma'am, I won't tell anybody in the world," he said.

Delivering along Webster, Albert was depressed. He thought he could still smell rancid butter. His spirits revived when he passed under a giant weeping willow overhanging Jerome Pindale's sidewalk. Jerome had warned the boy a half dozen times that he would take him before the justice of the peace if he caught him breaking branches from his tree. Today the door to the Pindale house was closed and the family automobile was gone. Albert couldn't resist. Standing in the stirrups, he broke off a nice switch.

He continued along Webster until he reached the Handleys' place on the edge of town. Returning, he took a shortcut across a vacant block where bunchgrass and cactus grew. He decided to change his daydream from kidnapping Paula to fighting Indians because the curved willow reminded him of a cavalry saber. He gave the mare a whack. She broke into a gallop, chiefly because the soil was soft and they were headed toward home.

The major threw a glance over his shoulder, satisfying himself that his troop galloped close behind. Their mood was sober, for they understood only too well the desperate odds they faced. Yet they did not slacken or hesitate. Clearly, they preferred death to retreat. Gold buttons gleamed on blue uniforms; banners snapped in the wind; sabers stood unsheathed. In the valley before them massed a frightful horde of Indians, faces painted, heads bedecked in war bonnets, hands gripping spears and rifles. With a nod of his head the major ordered the bugler to sound the charge. "On 'em, boys!" the major shouted, standing in his stirrups and lashing his frothing stallion. The troop thundered into the wall of Indians, sabers slashing, pistols firing, lungs expelling horrendous oaths. Though the slaughter was great on either side, the day belonged to the reckless line of blue. Uttering cries of injury and shame, the Indians suddenly turned and fled. When the mare trotted into Simmons Street, Albert felt entirely satisfied. Much booty had been recovered and many captives freed. Among the captives had been Paula, who for a brief moment before the daydream evaporated had ridden behind the major, her arms securely embracing him.

Halting the mare at the intersection of Simmons and Webster, Albert counted newspapers. He could see he would be two short. While he pondered whom among his remaining subscribers to deprive of a paper, he squinted into the setting sun and saw Mr. Handley's car pull into Webster. Mr. Handley was nearly blind and drove slowly so that others on the street could take notice and get out of his way. A moment later Albert saw a Model A skid into Simmons and head in his direction; it was Ralph Drayton and his buddies. Albert knew something would happen. He reined the mare around and retreated from the intersection. For a few seconds it was a hill that blocked Ralph's view of Mr. Handley's approach; then it was the setting sun in the far end of the street. The two automobiles collided with a terrific clang. Mr. Handley's car spun about and rammed into a power pole on the corner. Ralph's car careened across Samuel Darthenspogle's lawn, bounced onto his porch, took out three roof supports, and with a great splintering of wood buried its hood in the side of his garage.

Nobody seemed injured. Mr. Handley circled his car and the power pole muttering, "Why did they put that pole in the middle of the street?" Ralph Drayton sat on the running board of his immobilized car, his chin in his hands. "That old codger," he said. "Where in damnation did he come from?" His friends picked themselves off the driveway and fled through Darthenspogle's backyard.

In a few minutes Ross McCrimmon and his wife arrived, and while the deputy asked questions of Mr. Handley, Ralph, and Albert, his wife wrote answers in the black report book. A crowd gathered. One after another, people asked Albert, who had dismounted, to tell what had happened. Among the onlookers were Paula Ruckhart and her big brother. Paula said hello to Albert in a friendly manner and listened very respectfully while he told his story. She admired the mare and stroked her shoulder and neck. The mare tried to bite Paula, whereupon Albert gave the animal a cuff on the nose.

"Oh, don't hurt the poor thing," Paula said. "She's such a pretty horse. Would you take me for a ride on her some afternoon?"

"Gosh, yes," Albert said.

After it had got dark, he said he had to finish delivering his papers. He led the mare away until he was sure Paula wouldn't see how much trouble he had mounting. As he jumped into the saddle from the fender of a parked truck, it came to him where the missing papers were. He had forgotten that Cull Stevens and Garth Hazelton had picked up papers at the store. Jogging along toward their houses, he made up his mind he'd give the soggy paper to someone besides his own family. Considering all he had been through this afternoon, he believed he had the right to lie on the rug after supper and enjoy the comics from a dry newspaper. For a little while he daydreamed that he and Paula were married and had some children and sat respectably together in church every Sunday. It made him cheerful to remember how humble Ralph Drayton had become following the car accident. It also made him cheerful to think that maybe the Resurrection was going on all the time and that maybe, if folks took the trouble the next morning to open Walt Hampstead's coffin, they'd find it empty.

LEVI PETERSON, a native of Utah, is an award-winning writer of short stories. His collections *Canyons of Grace* and *Night Soil* have been widely praised. Many of his tales deal with rural life, with the complexities of being a Mormon, and with the elusiveness of morality in modern society. He is a professor of English at Weber State University in Ogden, Utah.

"I recall the classic parting words of my kinfolks as they left after Sunday dinner. 'We'll see you next Sunday, if the Lord wills and the creeks don't rise.' That was not just a homely cliche. It was a fact of life. The creeks could rise."

RECOGNITION OF AN ARTIST AND CAPTIVES

WILMA ELIZABETH McDANIEL

Recognition of an Artist

Big Muddy was too small for a real restaurant. All we had was Poor Boy's Cafe. It was tiny, with an L-shaped counter and four homemade tables and chairs. Mattie Willis opened it right after World War I. Her husband came home crippled and half-blind. The War Department conveniently lost his records or something. He never could get his pension started. *Mattie had to work.* All she knew was cooking hearty farmers' food. Today she would be known as a world-class chef. Her coffee was so special that farmers lingered for a cup before they left town. Of course a cup of coffee called for a piece of Mattie's delicious pie. Even Papa conceded that her pie was the next best thing to Mama's pie. No one could say more. I was too young to drink coffee, but I will always remember Mattie's hamburgers. The fatty aroma of sizzling beef and onions drifted down Big Muddy's one street. Buster sniffed the air and told me, "Wanda, this smells better than heaven." I asked him how he knew, because he had never been to heaven. He said, "We don't really know how good heaven smells or tastes, but we know how good Mattie's cooking smells and tastes." Well, I didn't argue with him, even though I was three years older. I couldn't honestly say that heaven smelled better than Mattie's cooking. Somehow, I thought it was *supposed* to, but I didn't want to get Buster riled up. Maybe the preachers could explain it to us later. They were wise and read up on these deep matters. I thought of a remark our schoolmate Chot Lee made about such matters. "If you don't know, just hunker down and keep your mouth shut."

About that time we had an incident occur that made a deep impression on our rustic lives. A young salesman from Tulsa had a flat tire on the outskirts of Big Muddy. At least everyone assumed he was a salesman. He wore a nubby tweed jacket and snapbrim hat and smoked a pipe. While he was getting the tire fixed, the service station attendant suggested he might like to get a bite to eat at our local cafe. It was noon and the cook would be serving lunch. The man thanked him and walked across the street to Poor Boy's. Mattie served him the specialty of the house, her Texas chili and large hamburger with homemade relish. She crowned her own culinary efforts with a thick slice of chocolate pie and her legendary coffee. The man paid his bill of thirty-five cents and thanked Mattie for a fine lunch. Two weeks later the *Tulsa World* ran a feature article on Poor Boy's Cafe. It turned out the suspected salesman was the human-interest reporter for the *World*. There was his story for all to read and re-live. He wrote that the most memorable meal he ever ate was in a hole-in-the-wall place called Poor Boy's Cafe. He said the food was a dozen times better than the Waldorf in New York or Maxim's in Paris. He had done assignments for both. He ended his article by saying America would be impoverished without the artistry and graciousness of women like Mattie Willis. We heard Mattie sat down at the counter and cried. She hadn't expected any special attention. Cooking well and being kind to people was as natural to her as breathing.

Of course the article became the talk of the township. Everybody wanted a copy for their family. Mr. Moon, the rural mailman, took up a collection and had the paper send us all of their unsold copies of that memorable Sunday issue. Papa tacked our copy of the article to the wall above the library table. It remained there until it turned yellow and brittle. In 1933 Buster got up on a chair and carefully took it down. He put it between the pages of an old hymnbook, so it would be safe on the long trip West. "We're leaving Big Muddy for good, but we're taking Poor Boy with us," he summed up for us all.

Captives

Weather actually controlled our lives in Big Muddy. I recall the classic parting words of my kinfolks as they left after Sunday dinner. "We'll see you next Sunday, if the Lord wills and the creeks don't rise." That was not just a homely cliche. It was a fact of life. The creeks could rise. They frequently did rise, with great inconvenience. Everyone had heard of the time old Sophie, the area's midwife, had to cross Big Muddy on a swinging bridge. She reached the expectant mother when the doctor in his new Model T Ford was helpless.

Weather could be very discomforting, cause frustration and disappointment. You take that Easter Sunday when we experienced a cloudburst and when it settled into steady light rain, we had to hide eggs in the straw of old man Creely's big barn. Maybe the rain was a blessing in one respect. Old Creely was a crotchety coot, but he must have been moved by the true spirit of Easter. He became the gracious host, spread down fresh hay, moved boxes and pieces of harness around, delighted all of us children, and astounded most of our parents by his abrupt change of attitude.

Wind could also be hard on us in Big Muddy Township. Sometimes it would carry on a vendetta with our neighbor to the north, Kansas. Sometimes Kansas would lash and beat the daylights out of Oklahoma. It could go on for days, dumping their best topsoil on us. I have seen it strike suddenly, catch us wherever we happened to be at that moment. It was really hard on chickens. I remember in March just after Saint

Patrick's Day, we were struck by the wind one afternoon. I went toward the mailbox and saw a couple of Mama's plump Orpington hens being buffeted by it. Caught unaware, their feathers blew up around them like flouncy dresses. One hen lost her balance and her dignity, and toppled over. Another blast of wind blew her up on the sheltered side of the tool shed. She huddled there safe all afternoon. Just before dark there was a lull in the wind, and the hens joined the other chickens on their perches. I remember the cows appeared content to be milked early.

The respite from the wind was brief. We had just started to eat supper when a fresh blast struck the farmhouse. The draft blew under the kitchen door and fluttered the flame of the kerosene lamp on the high stand. Uncle Garland passed the gravy. When the bowl came to my brother Rory, he spooned some on my mashed potatoes. The wind beat the trellises against the side of the house. Mama said, "We must secure those trellises to keep them from banging like that." She got up and took a fresh jar of yellow tomato preserves off the cupboard. "I forgot the other jar is almost empty." She opened it, turning the lid very expertly, then sat down again. The wind blew harder. Papa said, "Listen to that wind. Seems like we are getting everything they don't want up in Kansas. Worst part is, they can never decide to take it back. We're all captives of Mother Nature."

WILMA ELIZABETH McDANIEL is a native of Oklahoma. With her family, she migrated to California as a young woman and has since become a renowned poet as a result of books like *Sister Vayda's Song* (1982), *A Primer for Buford* (1990), and *The Girl from Buttonwillow* (1990). James D. Houston has called her writing "absolutely unique and magical." Eddie Lopez nicknamed her "the biscuits and gravy poet." She has also published many stories and memoirs.

"'That's right, my boy. Thirty minutes each day, minimum, and one day we'll be selling your records right here in this very store. Have your picture on the wall like those artists over there.'"

BLUE DANUBE WALTZ

ROBERT FRANKLIN GISH

After my first audition, Miss Matthews said, "We will begin with volume two in the Nick Manoloff series. It is available at May's Music Store downtown. I believe that's where you purchased your instrument, according to the bradded company logo on your case. You are clearly beyond the beginner stage, and yet . . . and yet you are not truly at the intermediate stage. The second volume of Mr. Manoloff's plectrum method should suit just fine. Your first lesson will be next Wednesday at 7:00 P.M. Please be prompt, Gilbert. We haven't much time."

I had dreaded meeting Miss Matthews. There were a lot of stories about her. Living the way she did. All her dogs. Her shack of a house. She wasn't at all like Jerry. So what if he was an alcoholic? So what if he showed up drunk for my lesson? But that's not what my mother said. "No nightclub derelict is giving my son guitar or any other kind of lessons. Not in my house. Not anywhere!" She really got on her high horse, "threw a royal fit," to use the words my father always used when his "old lady" was upset.

As for Miss Matthews, it hadn't been as bad as I had

thought it would be when my brother first parked in front of her decrepit little house on Gatewood. But I was eager for him to pick me up and, because of the reflection in the front window, had noticed him turn into the drive, hit the small ravine by her mailbox, and then cut the headlights, turn on the parking lights and wait in the red glow of a cigarette and, I knew for certain, the country music sounds of KOAT. He too had said, "Don't make me wait."

As I placed my guitar back in its case and said my good-byes I was more than ready to leave, although my fears had died down somewhat. The place really was shabby, outside, even in the dark. On the way across the yard I tripped on a big dog chain. Inside, the place was musty. Lots of overstuffed chairs and a big sofa with a bedspread over it. All in one small room—dominated by an ornately crafted, oak-cased, upright piano, with "Baldwin" naming it in gold decals. The floor was bare wood, with footpaths worn in it and with just one special carpet, a pretty Persian-looking one, under the piano bench. Her two dogs, a big collie-shepherd cross with a matted coat and a short-haired terrier of some kind, stayed in the kitchen. She wore at least two sweaters over her blouse and a long skirt that looked like it was made out of the same material as the curtains tied back and away from the front window.

Everything in the house smelled a bit mildewed. The house needed airing. And she did too. She was pale. She seemed almost totally colorless. The room and its furnishings seemed colorless too—except for the piano. And except for the last remnants of red in her graying hair. You could still tell that when she was young her hair had been red, or strawberry blond.

Closing the case, I noticed again the crack spreading out laterally from the end pin. Only a fraction of a fraction of an inch. I couldn't be sure how far. Couldn't really measure its marching advance. But its progress was inevitable—always there, bothering me, haunting me. Like death and the final coffin closing.

One moment of frustration. A slam of the instrument to the floor, driving the white plastic plug into the soft mahogany wood was all it took. A small, hairline crack at first. Then it started spreading. Then a major, visible crack.

Miss Matthews hadn't said anything about the crack when she had picked up my guitar and examined it, running her bony, big-veined hands with their tissue-paper skin across the strings, listening intently as they vibrated over the round sound hole, holding up the instrument to the light, cradling it in her lap. "This instrument is adequate, Gilbert," was all she said. She saw the scratches around the sound hole and beneath the half-moon, tortoiseshell pick guard. She saw the end-pin crack. She heard the difference it made. She had an ear for such things. Had to notice. Had to hear. She only frowned slightly, hesitated almost imperceptibly.

I hadn't told anybody about that crack. Not even Jerry. Not when it happened. Not when I first noticed it spreading slowly up and around the body, running with the grain of the wood, threatening to split the whole sound box and destroy the instrument. Render it dead in two useless pieces. "Hey, when did you crack your axe, Gillie? Better fix it," was all Jerry said. He saw it right away. But to repair it would announce its existence. Certainly I couldn't tell my father and mother. They had worked hard to put aside the $109 to buy the instrument, plus an extra $25 for the soft-shell case. Three dollars for the orange-and-black rope cord put on the guitar personally—neck nut to end pin—by Bernie May himself. Another dollar for polish. Both of them had gone with me, straight to Mr. May, to select just the right guitar for their boy, destined, they hoped, for a Decca or an RCA recording contract with the likes of the Tennessee Plowboy, Eddy Arnold.

"How do you like it, son? It's a beauty. Take good care of it and it will take you far. Could make you a fortune," beamed my father, and turned to shake hands with Mr. May.

"Oh, Gillie, you will practice hard, won't you?" chimed in my mother. "Early morning is the best time. When your mind is fresh and alert."

"That's right, my boy. Thirty minutes each day, minimum, and one day we'll be selling your records right here in this very store. Have your picture on the wall like those artists over there." And Mr. May pointed to glossy photographs of wide-hatted Western singers with their names signed across their guitars: "To Bernie," "Thanks, Bernie," "Best regards, Bernie," "Your pal." It was endless and impressive. Picture after picture after picture. Plus promotional posters! And the guitar was so beautiful in its newness and promise. Not a scratch on it. Not a blemish. The aroma of spruce top, rosewood neck, pearl dot inlay frets, soft-white purfling, glistening sunburst lacquer. I would practice. I would. People in cars, at home, in music stores would hear me.

Lessons with Jerry had been pretty easy. He showed me how to hold the guitar. Showed me how to crook my finger and place my thumb on the pick—the right size and thickness. Showed me some chords, wrote out some lyrics, to tunes like "Foggy River," "Anytime," "The Wabash Cannonball," "Tennessee Waltz." Showed me with penciled letters *C, F, G* or *D, G, A* when to change positions. It was fun. He would bring out his guitar and strum a few chords, do some fancy runs high up on the neck, and then pretty much go through some of the tunes he knew. He never insisted that I practice or anything like that. We just played some tunes together. Then he would light up a smoke and hang around for a cup of coffee and the $2.50 he charged for thirty-minute lessons.

But Miss Matthews was going to be more demanding. I could tell that as soon as I bought Nick Manoloff's *Guitar Method, Vol. II.* There he was on the cover, his hair slicked back—and he wore a tuxedo. Can you believe it? A tie-and-tails kind of guy. And the tunes in the book had names like "Over the Waves," "Long, Long Ago," "Volga Boat Song," things like that. There were scales for all the positions and all the keys and a bunch of notes and key signatures and foreign words. My folks wanted me to be like Eddy Arnold, not all the obscure guys whose pictures offered testimonial on the title page to Nick Manoloff and his stuffed-shirt guitar method.

When I handed it to Miss Matthews, she turned right away to two tunes pretty far into the book: "Denka Waltz" and one that went on for two or three pages—"The Blue Danube Waltz." Then she folded the book back so it would stay on her piano and started playing. Then she started singing some words to "The Blue Danube Waltz," all from memory, I guess. She really got carried away. Almost forgot I was there—playing her piano, singing along to this song I had never heard or heard about! Her back arched. She closed her eyes and pointed her face to the ceiling and didn't even look at the book after a bit. I was pretty uncomfortable. Then she stopped playing and sat silent for a moment, coming back from wherever she had been.

"We will play this as a duet, young man. It will be our goal. If you learn to play this you will always find enjoyment in your guitar. And you will be able to better understand other songs. I will teach you to play this song with feeling, as if you were dancing abroad to the orchestral arrangements of the immortal Strauss. Mr. Manoloff and I will usher you into the world of beauty, into the transportations of purist rhythm and melody. You will be caressed and refreshed in the waters of the Blue Danube."

I didn't know quite what to think. She was strange. Old Gene Laferink's mother, who had recommended Miss Matthews to my mother as a guitar teacher, had said that much. And Gene had confirmed it too, though he called her "wacky." The song, "Blue Danube Waltz," looked much beyond my skill level. Jerry had taught me some technique, I guess, but I was compelled to blurt out, "But I don't know how to read music."

"No mind, you will," was her reply, and we began that very night to supplement Mr. Manoloff's intermediate method book with lessons of Miss Matthews's own devising. When I asked why I couldn't play "Tennessee Waltz" or something like that instead, she simply stared at me with an expression of high disdain.

The routine began to take on a familiarity. My brother would drop me off and then pick me up, always waiting while she wrote out the next week's assignment. He would commiserate with me. And slowly we started making it, page after page, closer and closer to "Blue Danube Waltz." The fear of not practicing soon replaced the fear about the cracked condition of my guitar. I became friends with both of her dogs, who would come to greet me at the door and then retire back to their corner as my lesson began.

"Denka Waltz" came and went as first I accompanied her and then she accompanied me, each of us taking turns playing the melody and then chording. And there were some pretty difficult chords too, full-voiced chords, extended chords.

"Wonderful, Gilbert. We are almost to the Danube. Almost ready to cross."

That moment came early in October. She assigned "Blue Danube Waltz." And she prefaced it by saying, "This is what we have been working for. This is the song I wish you to play in next month's recital of my best students. We will play a duet!" I had to admit I had come to like some of Nick Manoloff's tunes—his arrangements for guitar and all. So I started working on the "Danube." We worked it out in three or four sections, learning one and then another, and then putting them all together. My fingers and wrists were stronger than they had ever been. Lessons were running longer and longer, forty-five minutes, an hour.

My brother rebelled and other family members had to pick me up—usually one of my parents or an aunt; even Willis Debke was enlisted one evening. Finally Miss Matthews judged me almost ready for the recital and, after nearly a year of study and practice, I did have "The Blue Danube Waltz" under technical control. "You still must feel the spirit of the song more deeply, Gilbert. Take your guitar to the river and play to the waters that dance about you. Imagine that water is not the brown, dirty water of the Rio Grande, but the rich, wonderful, blue water of the Danube."

I tried that. Walked about a mile down Bridge Street, and then down the big drainage ditch by La Vega Road, finally crossing through the bosque to the Rio Grande. I felt mainly the sand and the cracked clay and the pungent aroma of Russian olives and watched the shimmer of cottonwood leaves. Saw the sunlight glisten on the churning water.

My fingers knew all the notes, all the complicated chords. But I realized that I could never really feel the spirit of "The Blue Danube Waltz." What I felt was the spirit of the great river, the mighty Rio Grande, the water of my birthplace, coursing from Colorado headwaters through Texas and into the Gulf of Mexico. Rather than sorrow at some great loss, some embarrassment to Miss Matthews, I felt joy in realizing what I really felt—my river, my soul—and I played, instead, all the early songs Jerry had taught me, now embellished, to be sure, by more masterful melodic runs. I even cut loose with some Spanish tunes Rosendo

Abeyta had shown me one day in the park by the zoo. I had returned to my self. Recognized and returned to my musical home, my truer songs of the heart. Strangely, Mr. Manoloff and Miss Matthews had pointed a new direction, a new route back to my past, back to what I really was, really felt. Miss Matthews was right about one thing: you had to feel your music. She felt "The Blue Danube." But I didn't, . . . didn't feel "The Blue Danube Waltz" as she could hear it—out of who knows what past European ecstasies, past my playing, past my fretting and fingering there in her small house of memories.

The recital came and went. Barcelona School's cafeteria became an auditorium of approving parents—Miss Matthews's recital, their recital, not mine. We played our Danube duet. Even in her recital dress she couldn't shed the dinginess that surrounded her. I felt a tinge of sorrow, the sorrow youth has for age, as she again was transported, as she basked in the pride of parental applause.

On the ride home I told my parents about the crack, about the damage I had caused, frustrated in wanting to play more than I knew, more than I could. Told them that I wanted to trade guitars. Wanted a new kind of guitar, called a Fender "solid body." Told them that I couldn't really take more lessons from Miss Matthews. And that, for at least a time, I wanted to teach myself, play my own songs. Get with Gene and Rosendo and some guys at school and maybe form a little band.

"Good to hear you want to get back to the Eddy Arnold sound, son," said my father somewhat over his shoulder as he caught my eye in the rearview mirror.

"Don't worry about the crack to the guitar," volunteered my mother. "We can trade it in for something even closer to Eddy Arnold's. Mr. May will show us which one, I'm sure. He has photos of all the stars. But your duet was so pretty. And that waltz, that 'Blue Danube,' I liked it."

"Have you heard of Carl Perkins?" I asked, looking ahead in the street to see if we would make the traffic light, ". . . and a tune called 'Blue Suede Shoes'?"

ROBERT FRANKLIN GISH is a native of Albuquerque, New Mexico. He has published many articles and stories, as well as six books, including *Songs of My Hunter Heart, First Horses,* and *Frontier's End: The Life and Literature of Harvey Ferguson.* A member of the Cherokee Nation of Oklahoma, Gish is presently Director of Ethnic Studies at California Polytechnic State University in San Luis Obispo.

"The bars were my parents' living rooms. We spent our nights in them, our mornings in the Packard or a motor court."

RODEO LIFE

CYRA McFADDEN

Rodeo was used to announcers who treated the sport as a Wild West show, part vaudeville, part circus. Cy dignified it, with his ten-dollar words, his impeccably tailored, expensive suits, and his insistence that the cowboys were professional athletes. When he intoned "Ladies and gentlemen," women became ladies and men became gentlemen; the silver-tongued devil in the announcer's box, as often as not a rickety structure over the chutes and open to the rain, spoke with unmistakable authority. In a world where pretending to be an insider earns the outsider dismissal faintly underlined with menace, he counted as a working cowboy, though he earned his living with his mouth rather than his muscle.

Like the contestants, he lived from rodeo to rodeo, making just enough money to keep us in gas and hamburgers. He worked in all weather: heat, cold, freak rainstorms that turned arenas into mudholes. If he had extra money, everybody drank, and when we rented a room in a motor court, a luxury, cowboys bunked on the floor with their saddles for pillows. Despite his slight frame, he never hesitated about piling in when there was a fight; you had to get through him to get to somebody bigger, and because he was light on his feet and fast with his fists, few made it. Someone wading into my father also had to take on my mother, not one to sit on the sidelines letting out ladylike cries of dismay. A hundred-pound woman can do substantial damage with teeth, fingernails, and a high-heeled shoe, and Pat had an advantage going in. No man would hit her back, though she was swearing ripely and trying to maim him, because no self-respecting western man hits a lady.

The bars were my parents' living rooms. We spent our nights in them, our mornings in the Packard or a motor court—with Cy and Pat sleeping off their headaches and begging me to stop that goddamn humming—and our afternoons at the Black Hills Roundup or the Snake River Stampede, rodeos that blur into one.

Pat sat in the bleachers, if she wasn't trick riding. I sat in the crow's nest with Cy, sometimes announcing the Grand Entry or the national anthem for him or testing the p.a. system. "One two three four, testing testing testing." I wanted to be a movie star. Cy said you had to start somewhere.

The high point of those afternoons, for me, was when Cy played straight man for the rodeo clowns, who sometimes railed at him because he wouldn't allow off-color material, the crude jokes that were a staple. Not present just to entertain, the clowns also divert the bulls or horses when a rider is down. The cowboys and the crowd love and respect them. So did I, and when my father bantered with them from the stand, he took on added luster.

Pinky Gist and his two mules, Mickey and Freckles, George Mills, John Lindsay, the great Emmett Kelly, and a dozen others—sad-faced men in baggy pants, absurdly long shoes and long underwear, out in the arena, and my father aiding and abetting them:

"Eddie, there are ladies present here today. Would you mind pulling up your pants?"

"Sure, Cy." Eddie did a flawless double take, pulled his pants up, and doffed his porkpie hat to my father. When he lifted the hat, his pants fell down again, revealing long johns with a trapdoor.

"I'm sorry, Cy. I was asleep in the barrel over there and a train hit me. It tore the buttons off my suspenders."

"That wasn't a train, Eddie," Cy said, kingly at the microphone. "That was a two-thousand-pound Brahma bull, and there's another one coming out of the chute right now."

Eddie screamed hoarsely, stumbled across the arena, clutched at his pants and fell over his shoes. "I wondered why I never heard the whistle."

No matter how many times I heard these routines, they never paled for me. Such is the power of early-childhood conditioning that I still love slapstick; mine is the lone voice laughing at a club act in which the comic gets hit with a pie.

I'm less taken with exhibition roping. The great trick-rope artist on the circuit was Monty Montana, a handsome man who could do anything with a rope, including roping Cy Taillon's daughter. On my father's command, I pretended to be a calf; bolted through a string barrier and into the arena; ran like mad until Monty lassoed me, ran down his rope, threw me and tied me. He never hurt me. The crowd loved it. I hated it.

Not to be upstaged, Pat sometimes followed with her breakneck trick riding—headstands at the gallop, vaulting to the ground from a standing position in the saddle. She was so fearless that the cowboys gathered at the fence to watch her, wondering if this would be the night Cy's crazy wife killed herself.

I still have part of her trick-riding costume, a red Spanish bolero with white scrollwork, silver spurs with tooled-leather straps and canted-heel boots. The full-sleeved white satin shirt disappeared, as did the high-waisted red pants that would fit a twelve-year-old boy. Pat's life in those years is recorded in a few bits of her rodeo wardrobe, her own mutilated scrapbook, in which she also obliterated the supporting cast, and not much else.

Constants from those countless rodeos: the smell of sweat and horses that rose out of the open stalls, just below the booth; the fine dust that floated over the arena, powdering evenly cowboys, animals, the crowd, my father's suit and his pointy-toed boots; the haze of cigarette smoke over the stands; the whinnying of horses, the bawling of calves and howling of dogs, left in pickup trucks out in the parking lot.

Always present too were the high voices of women, wives and girlfriends and rodeo groupies, the "buckle bunnies" who were, and are still, the wives' natural enemies. They set the standards of female dress, with their starched curls and their pinkish pancake makeup, ending in a line at the chin. The buckle bunnies wore tight frontier pants and tooled-leather belts, into which they tucked their nailhead-studded shirts. One who was always around, and whom I admired, had a belt with beads spelling out her name, just above her neat rump: "Bonnee."

As for the wives, they were a tight-knit and wary bunch, sitting in the stands afternoon and night, watching their husbands compete and watching the single women through the smoke from their cigarettes. Those that had children left them sleeping in the trailers, and protected their primary interests. Cowboys then, and cowboys now, bear watching.

If the rodeo was in some two-dog town, we might be there for only one daytime and one evening performance, and then it was back on the road again, with a tour of the local bars in between. These had a certain classic similarity—a jukebox playing cowboy songs about lost love and lost illusions, beer signs with neon waterfalls, and on the wall the head of a deer with brown glass eyes.

Such bars did not bother to throw kids out, and so we played the pinball machines, or listened to the bragging and the laughter, or put our heads down on the table, among the shot glasses and beer bottles, and slept. Because slot machines were legal in Montana and Nevada, I liked the bars there best; they weren't legal for children, but who was watching? In Helena, Montana, with money I pried loose from my mother by practiced nagging, I won a jackpot. The quarters poured through my hands and onto the floor, a silver river of money.

No one would have thrown me out of the bars whatever I did, because I was Cy Taillon's daughter, his namesake, a miniature version of Cy in my own handmade boots and my Stetson.

Bartenders served my ginger ale with a cherry in it. Cowboys asked me to dance to the jukebox, and asked Pat if she knew my father had himself another little gal. Expansive on bourbon, Cy sat me on the bar and had me sing "Mexicali Rose." I have no voice, and hadn't then, but what I lacked in musicality, I made up for in volume. I could also imitate my father at the mike, booming out: "The only pay this cowboy is going to get tonight . . ." and other crowd pleasers.

Not only did rodeo people live like gypsies, traveling in an informal caravan from town to town; my father and I looked like gypsies, both dark-skinned to start with and tanned by the sun pounding down on us, both with dark hair and high cheekbones. Mine softened as I grew older. Cy's became more pronounced, until, just before he died, the flesh receded from the bone. Once, when I was ten, and he and I were having lunch in the Florence Hotel in Missoula, Montana, a woman asked to take a snapshot of us. She was from out of town, she said, and we were the first Indians she'd ever seen. We posed for her in front of the Florence's corny Indian murals, palms raised in the B movie "how" sign.

All of which I took for granted, when our family lived on the road, as the way everyone lived, though a social worker might have taken a dim view of it and I already knew at least one person who did. It was normal to have a dapper, charming father whose public self bore little resemblance to the private Cy, the one who drank too much and flared into an alcohol-fueled temper. It was normal to have a trick-riding, ex-chorus-girl mother who still did dancer's limbering-up exercises every morning, sinking into splits and sitting on the floor spraddle-legged, bending her head first to one knee and then to the other. "You better stay in shape when you grow up," she told me as I watched, "because a woman's looks are all she's got."

It was normal to spend days and nights at the rodeo, listening to Cy's molasses voice and the voices of the cowboys, jawing, swearing and bantering with each other, smelling leather, calves in their pens and horse manure; to sit high above the bleachers in the announcer's stand and all but melt with love and pride when, on cold nights, Cy took his jacket off and put it around me.

It wasn't just normal to live in a Packard, it was classy. A Packard was still a classy car when it was ankle deep in hamburger wrappers. Some rodeo people pulled trailers and thus had the equivalent of houses, but most drove pickups or the kind of cars which, if they were horses, would have been taken off and shot.

I also believed then that Pat would stay spirited and taut-bodied forever, like a young racehorse, and that my father, whenever he wanted to, could make himself invisible. He told me that he could, but not when anybody was watching, and in the somewhat deflected way he always told the truth, he was telling it then.

CYRA McFADDEN, distinguished novelist and essayist from Montana, is the daughter of famed rodeo announcer Cy Taillon and singer-dancer Pat Montgomery. This excerpt from *Rain or Shine* (1986), an autobiographical book that explores her parents' lives, suggests the transient if exciting nature of a young girl's life on the rodeo circuit. McFadden's hilarious 1976 novel, *The Serial,* which spoofed Marin County in California, is acknowledged to be at least a regional classic.

"He'd walk, steps measured as if the earth demanded measure, the willow fork held in both hands before him pointed at the ground like some kind of offering."

WATER WITCH

LOUIS OWENS

For a while, when I was very young, my father was a water witch. He took us with him sometimes, my older brother and me, and we walked those burned-up central California ranches, wherever there was a low spot that a crop-and-cattle desperate rancher could associate with a dream of wetness. The dusty windmills with their tin blades like pale flowers would be turning tiredly or just creaking windward now and then, and the ranch dogs—always long-haired, brown and black with friendly eyes—would sweep their tails around from a respectful distance. The ranches, scattered near places like Creston, Pozo, San Miguel, and San Ardo, stretched across burnt gold hills, the little ranch houses bent into themselves beneath a few dried-up cottonwoods or sycamores, some white oaks if the rancher's grandfather had settled early enough to choose his spot. Usually there would be kids, three or four ranging from diapers to hotrod pickups, and like the friendly ranch dogs they'd keep their distance. The cattle would hang close to the fences, eyeing the house and gray barn. In the sky, red-tailed hawks wheeled against a washed-out sun while ground squirrels whistled warnings from the grain stubble.

He'd walk, steps measured as if the earth demanded measure, the willow fork held in both hands before him pointed at the ground like some kind of offering. We'd follow a few yards behind with measured paces. And nearly always the wand would finally tremble, dip and dance toward the dead wild oats, and he would stop to drive a stick into the ground or pile a few rock-dry clods in a cairn.

A displaced Mississippi Choctaw, half-breed, squat and reddish, blind in one eye, he'd spit tobacco juice at the stick or cairn and turn back toward the house, feeling maybe the stirring of Yazoo mud from the river of his birth as if the water he never merely discovered, but drew all that way from a darker, damper world. Within a few days he'd be back with his boss and they'd drill a well at the spot he'd marked. Not once did the water fail, but always it was hidden and secret, for that was the way of water in our part of California.

When I think now of growing up in that country, the southern end of the Salinas Valley, a single mountain range from the ocean, I remember first the great hidden water, the Salinas River which ran out of the Santa Lucias and disappeared where the coastal mountains bent inland near San Luis Obispo. Dammed at its headwaters into a large reservoir where we caught bluegill and catfish, the river never had a chance. Past the spillway gorge, it sank into itself and became the largest subterranean river on the continent, a half-mile-wide swath of brush and sand and cottonwoods with a current you could feel down there beneath your feet when you hunted the river bottom, as if a water witch yourself, you swayed at every step toward the stream below.

We lived first in withdrawn canyons in the Santa Lucias, miles up dirt roads into the creases of the Coast Range where we kids squirmed through buck brush and plotted long hunts to the ocean. But there were no trails and the manzanita would turn us back with what we thought must be the scent of the sea in our nostrils. Rattlesnakes, bears, and mountain lions lived back there. And stories of mythic wild boars drifted down from ranches to the north. In the spring the hills would shine with new grass and the dry creeks would run for a few brief weeks. We'd hike across a ridge to ride wild horses belonging to a man who never knew that the kids rode them. In summer the grasses burned brown and the clumps of live oaks on the hillsides formed dark places in the distance.

Later we lived down in the valley on the caving banks of the river. At six and eight years we had hunted with slingshots in the mountains, but at ten and twelve we owned rifles, .22s, and we stalked the dry river brush for quail and cottontails and the little brush rabbits that, like the pack rats, were everywhere. Now and then a deer would break ahead of us, crashing thickets like the bear himself. Great horned owls lived there and called in drumming voices, vague warnings of death somewhere. From the river bottom we pinged .22 slugs off new farm equipment gliding past on the flatcars of the Southern Pacific.

Once in a while, we'd return to Mississippi, as if my father's mixed blood sought a balance never found. Seven kids, a dog or two, canvas water bags swaying from fender and radiator, we drove into what I remember as the darkness of the Natchez Trace. In our two-room Mississippi cabin, daddy longlegs crawled across the tar-papered walls, and cotton fields surged close on three sides. Across the rutted road through a tangle of tree, brush, and vine, fragrant of rot and death, was the Yazoo River, a thick current cutting us off from the swamps that boomed and cracked all night from the other shore.

From the Yazoo we must have learned to feel water as a presence, a constant, a secret source of both dream and nightmare, perhaps as my father's Choctaw ancestors had. I remember it as I remember night. Always we'd return to California after a few months, as much as a year. And it would be an emergence, for the Salinas was a daylight world of hot, white sand and bone-dry brush, where in the fall, red and gold leaves covered the sand, and frost made silver lines from earth to sky. Here, death and decay seemed unrelated things. And here, I imagined the water as a clear, cold stream through white sand beneath my feet.

Only in the winter did the Salinas change. When the rains came pounding down out of the Coast Range, the river would rise from its bed to become a half-mile-wide terror, sweeping away chicken coops and misplaced barns; whatever had crept too near. Tricked each year into death, steelhead trout would dash upstream from the ocean, and almost immediately the flooding river would recede to a thin stream at the heart of the dry bed, then a few pools marked by the tracks of coons, then only sand again and the tails and bones of big fish.

When I think of growing up in California, I think always of the river. It seemed then that all life referred to the one hundred and twenty miles of sand and brush that twisted its way northward, an upside-down, backwards river that emptied into the Pacific near Monterey, a place I didn't see till I was grown. As teenagers, my brother and I bought our own rifles, a .30-.30 and an aught-six, and we followed our father into the Coast Range after deer and wild boar. We acquired shotguns and walked the high coastal ridges for bandtail pigeon. We drove to fish the headwaters of the Nacimiento and San Antonio rivers. And from every ridge top we saw, if not the river itself, then the long, slow course of the valley it had carved, the Salinas. Far across were the rolling Gabilan Mountains, more hawk hills than mountains, and on the valley bottom, ranches made squares of green and gold with flashing windmills and tin roofs.

After school and during summers we worked on the ranches, hoeing sugar beets, building fences, bucking hay, working cattle (dehorning, castrating, branding, ear-clipping, inoculating, all in what must have seemed a single horrific moment for the bawling calf). We'd cross the river to drive at dawn through the dry country watching the clumps of live oak separate from the graying hillsides. Moving shadows would become deer that drifted from dark to dark. Years later, coming home from another state, I would time my drive so that I reached that country at daybreak to watch the oaks rise out of night and to smell the damp dead grasses.

Snaking its way down through our little town was a creek. Dipping out of the Coast Range, sliding past chicken farms and country stores, it pooled in long, shadowed clefts beneath the shoulders of hills and dug its own miniature canyon as it passed by the high school, beneath U.S. 101, around the flanks of the county hospital and on to the river where it gathered in a final welling before sinking into the sand. En route it picked up the sweat and stink of a small town, the flotsam and jetsam of stunted aspirations, and along its course in tree shadow and root tangle, under cutbank and log, it hid small, dark trout we caught with hook and handline. From the creek came also steelhead trapped by a vanished river, and great blimp-bellied suckers which hunkered close to the bottom, even a single outraged bullhead which I returned to its solitary pool. At the place where the chicken-processing plant disgorged a yellow stream into the creek, the trout grew fat and sluggish, easily caught. We learned every shading and wrinkle of the creek, not knowing then that it was on the edge already, its years numbered. I more than anyone, fisher of tainted trout, kept what I thought of as a pact with the dying creek: as long as the water flows and the grass grows.

Up on Pine Mountain, not so much looming as leaning over the town of my younger years, a well-kept cemetery casts a wide shadow. From this cemetery, one fine summer evening, a local youth exhumed his grandmother to drive about town with her draped across the hood of his car, an act so shocking no punishment could be brought to bear. Later, when I asked him why, he looked at me in wonder. "Didn't you ever want to do that?" he asked. That fall, after a bitter football loss, members of the high school lettermen's club kidnapped a bus full of rooters from a rival school, holding them briefly at gunpoint with threats of execution. The summer before, an acquaintance of mine had stolen a small plane and dive-bombed the town's hamburger stand with empty beer bottles. The town laughed. Later, he caught a Greyhound bus to Oregon, bought a shotgun in a small town, and killed himself. It was that kind of place also. Stagnant between Coast Range and river, the town, too, had subterranean currents, a hot-in-summer, cold-in-winter kind of submerged violence that rippled the surface again and again. Desires to exhume and punish grew strong. Escape was just around a corner.

Behind the cemetery, deep in a wrinkle of the mountain, was an older burial ground, the town's original graveyard, tumbled and hidden in long grasses and falling oaks. Parting the gray oat stalks to read the ancient stone, I felt back then as astonished as a Japanese soldier must have when he first heard the words of a Navajo code talker. Here was a language that pricked through time, millennia perhaps, with painful familiarity but one that remained inexorably remote.

A year ago, I drove back to the house nine of us had lived in on the banks of the river. The house was gone, and behind the empty lot the river had changed. Where there had been a wilderness of brush and cottonwoods was now only a wide, empty channel gleaming like bone. Alfalfa fields swept coolly up from the opposite bank toward a modern ranch house. "Flood control," someone in the new Denny's restaurant told me later that afternoon. "Cleaned her out clear to San Miguel," he said.

LOUIS OWENS, who was raised in California's Salinas Valley, is a novelist, essayist, and noted scholar. He is professor of English at the University of New Mexico. *The Sharpest Sight* (1991), his first novel, has received widespread acclaim. Owens is also an acknowledged expert on the writing of John Steinbeck, and he has written a book titled *John Steinbeck's Re-Vision of America.*

GROWTH OF
COMMUNITY

*"Roy's parents had never gotten over the surprise of becoming
parents when they were nearly fifty years old. They shrugged in
confusion as he ruled them and terrorized the neighborhood."*

THE NEW SIDEWALK

DOROTHY BRYANT

"No. I want it smooth." Louie Rocca thrust his belly forward and shook his head. "Smooth, like glass."

"Yeah, but you know, it gets a little wet from the rain, somebody's going to slip and break their neck."

"What's the matter? You can't do it smooth? You don't know how?"

The workman flushed. "Don't worry, mister. I'll make it like frosting on a cake." He inched his kneeboards further forward on the wet concrete. As he bent and reached for his trowel, I heard him mumble, "And I hope you fall on your fat ass some foggy morning."

I stood leaning on the wooden barricade with the other children and watched him work. His right arm smoothed the metal trowel back and forth over the thick gray ooze in a long sideways figure eight. Bubbles and swirls erased as he ironed them out in steady, rhythmic movements.

"And you kids, you keep off it, see?" I jumped at the sound of Louie Rocca's voice behind me, and, as I turned, my nose almost hit his belly. I looked up at his face, trying to match his hard look with a defiant look of my own.

I knew the other kids were watching, and Louie Rocca was our enemy. We never played ball in front of his house; if the ball went up over his roof to his backyard, he would keep it and say that would teach us to keep away from his property. There were so many children on the block that someone's father was always replacing a broken window. We had broken his window only once, and that time it had been his own son Dominic who was at bat. Dominic, to our surprise, had been terrified and had sworn on the Blessed Virgin that he hadn't done it; his father believed him and called us criminals, destroyers of property who would all end up in prison someday.

He pointed his finger at me. "First kid who touches it before it's dry, I'll use a two-by-four on him."

I moved away from him, but Roy stood still and stared back at him through his thick glasses. "Who's going to touch your lousy old sidewalk? Besides, my father says you touch me and he'll get the police on you."

"Hah. Sure, the police. They know you, huh, Roy? The young Mafia, that's what we got on this block."

He was right about the police knowing Roy. Roy's parents had never gotten over the surprise of becoming parents when they were nearly fifty years old. They shrugged in confusion as he ruled them and terrorized the neighborhood. Once he had thrown a lighted firecracker into our mailbox, starting an interesting, if small and quickly quenched, fire. The BB gun he received one Christmas turned him into the neighborhood sniper. The police had taken the gun from him, and he turned to knife throwing. An accident ended this phase before he managed to hurt anyone but himself. He had been practicing throwing his knife against a fence. The handle of the knife hit the fence, and the knife bounced back, hitting Roy in the left eye. Three operations had saved his sight, but he now wore thick glasses. The experience had not changed him, and the glasses, instead of making him look studious or vulnerable, only made his fierce eyes look bigger. No one ever called him four-eyes.

Louie Rocca turned away and began to walk around the wooden barricades as he had been doing since the concrete had been dumped. For an hour he harassed the finisher, talking about pitch and drainage and joints while the man did his work. He smiled only when adults stopped to watch. Then he would point to the square in front of his house. No halfway patch jobs for him, he would say. Rip the whole thing out and do it right, he repeated over and over. His words implied an affluence rare in 1938, when the other fathers on the block were patching and painting only when necessary, counting themselves lucky to have met their last payment on the mortgage.

The adults would nod and walk on. We children were the only constant audience, and we gave all our attention to the workman, asking him questions and envying his being paid for enjoying such an orgy of mud molding. Finally he finished, cleaned his tools, and loaded them onto his truck, saying, "Just keep off of it till tomorrow."

Louie Rocca nodded impatiently and looked relieved as the man drove away. Then he turned and looked at the slick surface, delicately jointed in neat squares. Now it was all his. He owned the best sidewalk on the block. The other children had been called in to dinner, but Roy and I still leaned on the wooden barricade.

"What you waiting for? Go home. You kids go home."

I moved one foot, but Roy stood still, as if he had heard nothing. Louie Rocca moved closer. "You think I don't know why you hanging around? Soon as my back is turned you figure to write your name or some dirty thing on my sidewalk." He walked carefully across a plank to the front steps and sat down. "You might as well forget it; I'm going to sit right here and keep an eye on you."

Roy nudged me, and we turned and started walking slowly up the block.

"How long do you think he'll stay there?" I asked.

"I don't know. He can't sit there all night, can he?" Roy smiled. "See you later." He ran up the stairs and into his house.

I could hear my father washing in the bathroom as I walked into the kitchen. My mother turned from the stove.

"You're late. Dinner's ready. Wash your hands."

I washed my hands at the kitchen sink and dried them on a dishtowel. My father came into the kitchen and we sat down. My mother ladled pale yellow broth into our soup plates.

"I was watching the man put in the concrete," I explained.

"Is it finished?" asked my mother.

"Yes," said my father. "A nice job too. I saw it on my way home. Slick as glass." He laughed. "That guy don't know what he's letting himself in for. The way he hates the kids playing around his place. Why, when those kids see how smooth that is for roller skating, they're going to play all their hockey games right smack in front of his house."

I hadn't thought of that. Where had I left my skates? I began to eat faster. I wanted to suggest the hockey game to Roy before someone else got the idea—and the credit.

My mother sighed. "I don't know what that man has against the kids. It's a disgrace, a grown man yelling at them the way he does."

"He's a big bully, that's what."

"Eat your soup," said my mother.

"He likes to be the boss, all right," said my father. "He runs that house of his like he was Mussolini himself."

"And he gets to look like him more every day," said my mother. "His wife and the kids too. They're all round as barrels. Why, his wife told me he has a fit if they don't have pasta at every meal. I can cook as good as she . . ."

"Sure, you can. Sure."

"We don't prove anything by stuffing ourselves."

"He told me if you would fatten me up I wouldn't catch so many colds," I said.

"I guess I know how to feed my family without that big mouth telling me." The bowl of stew clattered as she set it down hard on the table.

"Take it easy," said my father.

"It makes me mad. All I ever hear from them is they got this and they got that. The only time they ever ask you into the house is to show you some new thing they got, and how they got such a good price because they know this guy and that guy, and you stand there and listen to all that big talk and they don't even offer you a chair and a glass of wine. You know all the time they haven't got any more than we have."

"He likes to be the big man, all right," said my father.

"Big man," said my mother. "I'm sick and tired of hearing what a big man he is. And how many acres he had in the old country. And how many men worked for him in the grape season. And how many rich people from Torino came to buy his wine. If he was such a big man, why didn't he stay there?"

"I heard it was his father's place," said my father. "And when he died, everything went to the oldest son. He and Louie didn't get along so well . . ."

"I can see why."

". . . and he finally kicked Louie off the place. At least that's what I heard."

"Can I go out now, Mom?" I asked. "I'm finished."

"What about your homework?"

"No homework tonight."

"After the dishes. Just till it gets dark. Don't forget to put on a sweater. It's not summer anymore."

I hurried through the dishes while my mother put the leftover stew in the icebox and swept the kitchen floor. Louie Rocca probably was inside eating. I didn't want Roy to get to the concrete before I did. I hung the dishtowel on the rack, grabbed my sweater, and ran.

Some of the children were already playing one-foot-off-the-gutter, but I shook my head when they called me. I ran to the wooden barricade, where Roy was already standing.

Louie Rocca was still sitting on the steps. Next to him was a greasy plate with a fork and one or two strands of spaghetti on it, and a half-filled glass of red wine. He had eaten his dinner on the steps. As I reached the wooden barricade, I saw something resting across his knees.

"That's right, kid. See? I got my shotgun here. I'm gonna shoot the first little bastard touches my sidewalk."

"You don't dare shoot me," said Roy.

"No?" He picked up the gun.

I pulled at Roy's arm. "Come on. Let's get in the game. I have to go in when the streetlights go on." Roy let me pull him away, but he wouldn't play. He just sat on the curb until his mother called. As he waved good night, the streetlights went on. Louie Rocca was still sitting on the steps holding the gun when I went into the house.

"He's got a shotgun," I told my mother as I undressed. "And he's going to sit there and watch. And anybody touches his sidewalk, he's going to shoot them dead."

"Did you hear that?" my mother said. "That crazy man. He's going to hurt someone."

My father did not answer, but I heard him open and close the front door. I got into bed and my mother turned off the light. In a little while I heard the front door open and close again, and I heard my father speak.

"It's all right. It isn't loaded. He showed me. But he says he's going to sit out there all night until the concrete is hard. He's afraid one of the kids will mess it up or a cat might walk across it or something. It's his business. Let's go to bed."

All night I dreamed of Louie Rocca. He was standing on his steps holding his shotgun. On each step behind him was a row of balls. One of the balls I recognized. It was the one I had lost over his roof a few weeks before. I was standing with sixteen other children, surrounding the fresh concrete. The wooden barricade was gone, and each of us had a toe touching the edge of the wet sidewalk. Roy was standing next to me. I looked down and saw that he was wearing roller skates. We began to chant, "Give us the ball, Louie, give us the ball."

He raised the gun with his right hand and with the other hand pointed to the balls. "I got fifty acres of the best grapes," he shouted. "Count them. Anybody tries to take one, I'll shoot him."

Roy crouched, then pushed himself forward. He spread out his arms and glided in a wide arc on one skate across the soft gray surface, cutting a deep track, and stopping in front of Louie Rocca. Louie raised the gun, pointed it at Roy, and pulled the trigger. From the gun oozed a string of greasy spaghetti which slid down the front of Louie's shirt. Then the balls began to roll down the steps. I looked at the sidewalk; it had turned into a sheet of glass. As the balls bounced down the steps, each one cracked the glass with a sharp clink, clink.

Clink, clink. The sound came from the kitchen. The edges of the window shades were light. I dressed as fast as I could, not stopping to tie my shoes.

"Where are you going?" asked my mother as I ran through the kitchen. "Breakfast isn't ready yet."

"I'll be right back." I ran out the front door. I was still half in my dream and almost believed that I would find glass in front of Louie Rocca's house. I ran down the front steps. As I reached the sidewalk I looked down the block and saw that there were, as in my dream, a group of children surrounding the square in front of the Rocca house. I looked for Roy, but he was not with them. Louie Rocca was still sitting on his front steps with the shotgun across his knees. His head was resting against the banister. He was asleep. With his eyes closed his face was softer. The thick cheeks seemed to sag and his mouth looked sad, as if he had unhappy dreams. None of the children moved. They were all watching Louie Rocca and seemed to be almost holding their breath.

When I reached the wooden barricade and looked down at the concrete, I saw why. Almost every inch of the new sidewalk was etched and lined. There were footprints in circles. There were pictures: a horse, a gun, a sailing ship, a house with a curl of smoke coming out of the chimney, a knife, a firecracker exploding, a tree. Neatly lettered along the curb was the entire alphabet. Across the middle of the sidewalk, gouged in letters a foot high, were the words LOUIE ROCCA IS A BIG FAT WOP.

No one said a word. As I turned to look at the faces of the other children, I saw Roy across the street, standing in front of his house. I called to him, "Roy, look." But he only smiled and went back into his house.

I heard a clattering noise and looked back. Louie must have heard me. He had moved, and the gun fell off his knees. As he opened his eyes, the children ran. I ran too.

Years later, Louie Rocca's sons replaced the concrete, but for as long as we lived there the sidewalk remained as it was. Neighbors averted their eyes as they passed it, and looked up or to the side if they had to walk over it. We children never mentioned it, even among ourselves.

For a time we avoided Roy. Such a permanent symbol of public defeat was, I suppose, more than any of us had wanted. Perhaps we had some vague concept of fair play extending even to an enemy.

Roy and I drifted apart. He had taken to using his knife on whatever small animals he could capture. That and schoolwork began to absorb him and, I guess, led to his later success. He's a famous surgeon now, but I wouldn't want him to operate on me.

DOROTHY (CALVETTI) BRYANT was raised in San Francisco. For a quarter-century, she has been one of California's most productive writers. Moreover, as *San Francisco Chronicle* book editor Patricia Holt points out, Dorothy has "consistently and amazingly anticipated the events and issues of her time." Among her celebrated novels are *Ella Price's Journal* (1972), *A Day in San Francisco* (1983), and *The Test* (1992). She has also written significant nonfiction and drama.

" 'Be careful with those tools, my lads. See this?' he tugged at the patch that covered his eye. 'A stray screwdriver can put your eye out!' "

MAL DE OJO

GERALD W. HASLAM

My grandmother really didn't want me hanging around Mr. Samuelian's yard, but I did anyways. He was the old poet who lived next door to Abuelita and me, and for some reason she didn't like him; she said he was crazy, but us guys all loved him. He was the only grown-up in the neighborhood who treated us like friends, not kids. That week me and Flaco Perez and Mando Padilla we were working with him on a big birdhouse—"a hotel for our little friends," he called it.

"Friends!" huffed Grandma when I told her. "Those birds eat my garden. They leave the nasty white spots! First that mad Armenian *feeds* them, and now he *houses* them. He is *loco!*" She sounded genuinely agitated.

"They're just birds, Abuelita," I pointed out.

"You have no idea the damage they do. Like that crazy Armenian, they are a menace."

What could I say? "Okay."

"I warn you, *mijito*. Avoid that Armenian. He is *peligroso.*"

"Dangerous?"

"He reads all those books."

"Oh," I said.

Abuelita prided herself in being plainspoken. My father had once said to me, "Your grandmother not only calls a spade a spade, she calls a lot of other things spades too."

She had not liked the poet much since that first day when he'd moved into the neighborhood and she'd asked if he wasn't an Armenian. He said no, his parents had been Armenians but he was an American, born and raised in Fresno. That answer displeased Abuelita, who always identified people by nationalities . . . or her version of nationalities, anyways.

Mr. Samuelian, in response, asked what nationality she was and, like always, my grandma said, "Spanish."

"Spanish," he grinned, "what part of Spain are you from?"

Abuelita really didn't like that—the words or the grin—since she, like me, had been born in Bakersfield. "My *people* were from Spain," she spat. What's funny is that my Mom told me our family came from Mexico.

"*Voy a pagarlo en la misma moneda,*" Abuelita had mumbled after that encounter, but I didn't understand what she meant, something about paying him the same money. My father was a gringo and he hadn't let my momma use much Spanish around me—before they got divorced, I mean—and I had come to live with my grandma so Momma could go to L.A. and find a good job.

Anyways, me and Flaco and Mando were working on the hotel that next afternoon while Mr. Samuelian was at the library. We were finishing it up, really, when a big shiny car swooped into the dirt driveway of the yard. Since our neighbor owned only a bicycle, I had rarely seen an automobile here.

A husky man who favored Mr. Samuelian, but real suntanned like he worked outside all the time, he swung from the door. He had the same burst of white hair, the same hook of a nose; his eyebrows were black and he had a ferocious black mustache. One of his eyes was covered by a dark patch. "Hello, my lads!" he called. "Where is Sarkis Samuelian?"

"He went to the library," I answered.

"Always reading. He will destroy his vision yet. And who are you young men?"

"I'm Gilbert. I live next door. This is Flaco and Mando."

"Well, young gentlemen, I am Haig Samuelian, brother of Sarkis Samuelian. And what do you work on?"

"It's just this birdhouse," Mando answered.

"Be careful with those tools, my lads. See this?" he tugged at the patch that covered his eye. "A stray screwdriver can put your eye out!"

"Oh!" I said involuntarily. I'd heard all my life about the variety of implements that might put an eye out, but this was my first contact with someone to whom it had actually happened.

Before I could inquire further, the poet returned toting a load of books. "Ahhh!" he called. "My little brother visits! Why aren't you in Fresno counting your raisins?"

"Only a fool counts his raisins and ignores his grapes!" responded the one-eyed man, and he hugged Mr. Samuelian. "I've just been commiserating with your associates here."

"Oh," grinned our neighbor, "these young scamps. They're doing a fine job on the new birdhouse, though. Come in, Haig, we must have coffee. How's Aram? Where is Malik's son now? And Dorothy, still a dancer?" They disappeared into the house.

As soon as they were gone, Flaco said, "That guy I think he got his you-know-what poked out."

We enlivened the remainder of the afternoon discussing his poked eye. "I wonder what's left. I wonder is it just a hole there," said Mando.

"Maybe it's all dried up like Mrs. Lopez's dried-up old hand," Flaco suggested.

"Grossisimo!" It was a word we'd invented, so we giggled together.

"Maybe it's like that place where there use to be a boil on your brother Bruno's neck," I told Mando.

"Grossisimo!" he said.

Before we went home that night, Haig Samuelian handed each of us a small bag of pomegranates. "Those are from Fresno, my lads. They are the finest in the world."

"Gee, thanks."

I took mine to Grandma, but she would not touch them. "You got these from that Armenian *pirata?* Him with his *mal de ojo?*"

"Bad of eye?" A lot of the stuff she said in Spanish wasn't clear to me.

"The *evil* eye, *mijito,* the *evil* eye."

"Evil eye? Abuelita, that's just Mr. Samuelian's brother . . ."

"Another of those Armenians!" she hissed.

". . . and he got that eye poked out by a screwdriver."

"You are young," she told me. "You haven't seen behind that mask. You do not understand the realm of evil."

"The realm of evil?"

She stopped then and gazed directly at me. "If you ever look deeply into *un mal de ojo* you will see Hell itself."

"Hell itself?" I didn't have a clue what she was talking about.

"Pray your rosary," she cautioned.

"Okay."

"And don't be working outside in the sun with those two *malcriados,*" she added.

"Why?"

"It will make you dark like a *cholo.* You must wear a hat, *mijito.*"

Like a *cholo?* That's the name the guys at school called all the kids—mostly Indians—who'd just come from Mexico. Hey, I *wanted* to be dark like them so I wouldn't look different from the other kids in my class. At Our Lady of Guadalupe School, I was the only Ryan amidst Martinezes and Gonzalezes and Jiminezes. I'll tell you a secret: One day, when Abuelita wasn't home, I even put black shoe polish on my hair, but it looked real dopey. I had a heck of a time washing it out before she got back.

Anyway, the morning after our *cholo* talk I couldn't wait to dash outside into the sunlight and slip over to our neighbor's yard, maybe steal a glance behind that patch. The large car was still there, but its owner wasn't in sight, so I helped Mr. Samuelian water his weeds. Then he busied himself reciting his latest verse—"Great unconquered wilderness is calling, calling me! Its crystal peaks and wooded glens all yearn to set me free!"—while staking up peas. Before long, the man with a hole in his face emerged from the small house and began picking and sampling ripe plums from a tree in the overgrown yard. "These are wonderful," he said, "almost as good as the ones in Fresno."

After a moment, his tone deepened: "You see those sharp stakes Sarkis carves. Beware of them! My eye . . ." he said heavily, pulling at his patch.

I gulped.

Later that day, me and Mando and Flaco we were erecting the bird hotel when this big mean kid named David Avila, who had chased us home from school more than once, he swaggered up and stood on the dirt border between the yard and the pitted street. A week before he'd caught me and given me a Dutch rub and a pink belly too; he especially liked to pound my pale skin because it turned red so easily. Avila he looked like a large brown toad and he was almost that smart, but he had real biceps and the beginnings of a mustache. Only a year ahead of us at Our Lady of Guadalupe School, he was already a teenager.

Anyways, the big toad he kind of studied us, sneered, then hollered, "Hey, leettle *pendejos,* I can't wait for them birds. I got me a BB gun and I'll keell 'em all. Maybe I'll shoot you three leettle *pendejos* too. You just wait!"

"No, *you* just wait, young criminal!" I heard a shout, and Mr. Samuelian's brother dashed from the plum tree's foliage—I don't think Avila had noticed him there. In a moment, he had the bully by the neck and was shaking him with one hand while he thrust an open wallet into his face with the other. "Do you see this badge?" he demanded. "I'll have you in jail for *years* if you bring a BB gun around here! Do you understand? Do you see this patch? A BB gun!" He shook Avila again.

The bully had wilted quickly under Haig Samuelian's storm, and once released, he scurried away.

"Scalawag!" the one-eyed man shouted after him. "Scoundrel," he continued fuming as he returned, his fierce mustache twitching. "I can have him jailed!" He thrust his wallet toward us and displayed a small badge that said, "Friend of the Fresno County Sheriff's Department."

"Ah, Haig! Haig!" called Mr. Samuelian, emerging from his pea patch to pound his brother's back. "Ever the crusader!"

"BB guns!" said Haig Samuelian, and he spat vehemently on the ground and jerked his patch momentarily.

"Come," urged Mr. Samuelian, "let me give you a glass of tea, Haig," and they entered the small house.

"I bet it's a glass eye under that patch is what," said Mando. "I tried to look under when he was pickin' plums, but I couldn't see nothin'.'"

"I think it's a big ol' bloody hole," suggested Flaco.

"With worms, maybe," I added. "I'll bet there's big worms in it."

"Grossisimo!" chorused my pals.

I joined my grandma talking to our other neighbor, Mrs. Alcala, when I arrived home for dinner. "Esperanza, you didn't actually *eat* the pomegranates that *brujo* gave you?" Abuelita demanded.

"Of course," smiled old Mrs. Alcala, who was Flaco's grandmother. "They were delicious. And he's not a *brujo,* Lupe, he's just another Samuelian, a gentleman but . . . ah . . . *very* enthusiastic."

"Enthusiastic?"

"And very friendly," added Mrs. Alcala.

"*Two* of those Armenians now," my grandma said. "Both of them *loco.*"

Mrs. Alcala was smirking when she added, "The Samuelians aren't the only *locos* in this neighborhood."

"And what is *that* supposed to mean, Esperanza?"

"Oh, nothing," replied the old woman, grinning as she hobbled away on two canes. "Hasta la vista, Lupe."

That long, warm evening the Samuelian brothers sat in wooden lawn chairs talking, and after Grandma freed me from chores I wandered over to listen. "That was the day I fought Dikran Nizibian, the terror. Remember, Sarkis? I fought him for an hour and fifteen minutes nonstop, the longest and fiercest battle in the history of Fresno. We fought all the way up Van Ness Avenue to Blackstone, and then we fought for a mile down Blackstone. Our sweat flowed through the gutters. The police stood back in awe to watch such a battle. Businesses closed. Priests held crosses to their hearts. Doctors averted their eyes. Strong women prayed. Strong men fainted."

"Who won? Who won?" I asked, breathless.

"Who won?" he paused. Mr. Samuelian's brother twitched his mustache and tugged his patch. "I'll tell you who won. Do you see this eye?"

he pointed at the cloth covering his empty socket. "The evil Dikran Nizibian tried to *gouge* it out in the middle of Blackstone Avenue in Fresno forty years ago, but . . ." another pause, another twitch, another tug . . . "he regrets it to this day because I knew a secret: Never use more when less will do! Never use two when one will do! I had saved my final strength. With it, I threw the ruthless Nizibian from me and broke everything on him that could be broken. I broke several things that *couldn't* be broken. He never fought again, did he, Sarkis?"

"Not that I remember," replied Mr. Samuelian.

"He never bullied anyone again."

"Not that I remember."

"Nizibian the terror was finished," Haig Samuelian nodded with finality, pulling absently at his patch.

"*Gouged* his eye out," I mumbled as I wandered home.

I told my pals the story of the great Fresno fight the next day at school. We were all eager to hurry back that afternoon and hear more from Mr. Samuelian's brother. On our way, however, while discussing the vast pit that had been gouged in Haig Samuelian's face by the evil Nizibian, and hoping at last to catch a glimpse of its depths, we spied David Avila striding toward us. Oh, no! We immediately began sprinting, each in a different direction, in the hope the bully might be confused.

Unfortunately for me, he wasn't. I was the only blond at Guadalupe School, so when Avila selected a target, I was usually his first choice. I didn't feel honored by that. I didn't have time to feel anything but scared because I was too busy sprinting. The bully was after me at a dead run. Although I was carrying my slingshot, it never occurred to me to use it because I was too busy trying to escape.

I was pretty fast for a little kid, and I got even faster with David Avila on my tail, so at first I kept him way behind me. I was sprinting and glancing back, sprinting and glancing back, juggling my book bag. Before long, though, I realized that Avila the terror was closing the gap between us, his toad eyes slits of rage. I worked even harder to escape, but my breath was growing hot and shallow and my thighs were beginning to tighten and burn.

I shot another look behind me, and he was so close that I saw the shadow of a mustache on his upper lip and the pink pimples decorating his bronze chin. My breath was searing me and my knees couldn't seem to lift anymore; my book bag swung wildly from side to side.

Just as I turned the corner of my block, I lost control of my book bag and it dropped, spilling its contents. I was nearly safe, but if I didn't pick up my things I'd never see them again—and I knew the evil Avila had to be reaching for me.

Hesitating over my books and papers, I glanced back despondently, ready for the twisted arm, the Dutch rub, or the pink belly that was certain, and to my astonishment I realized that Avila had halted. He thrust his hands into his pockets and turned away. When I spun around, I saw the one-eyed Samuelian standing in front of his brother's yard, hands on hips, glaring at David Avila. When I peered once more at the bully, he was retreating rapidly.

I was so relieved that I almost forgot to pick up my books and papers. When I finally did, though, I hurried to our neighbor's house. The large car was being loaded with a suitcase, and Haig Samuelian said to me, "Remember, never use more when less will do, and that young hoodlum will soon learn to leave you alone."

Then the two older men returned to what seemed to be a conversation in progress. "No matter, Sarkis," the younger brother said. "I'll pass the message on to Aram. He will understand." The men hugged, then Haig Samuelian noticed what I carried and said, "Don't let this young man play with that slingshot. You remember my eye, don't you?" He pointed toward his empty socket as he swung into the driver's seat.

His brother smiled, "I remember."

"Well, I must be on my way. I have grapes to tend in Fresno." The two brothers shook hands. The larger man tugged his patch and smiled out the window as he started the engine. "Farewell, young man," he said to me.

I didn't reply because I'd noticed something a moment before when Haig Samuelian had tugged at his small mask while sitting there, his face level with mine. I noticed that there was no fair, untanned skin beneath the patch or the string that tied it.

No fair skin.

Beneath the wristwatch Abuelita had given me last Christmas my own surface was pale as a baby's. Then I realized what that had to mean: "You been changin' eyes!" I thought aloud.

"What is that?" the driver inquired.

"Your patch, it's on the other eye. You been changin' eyes," I spoke as I began to realize what had to have been happening: "You been changin' every day."

Haig Samuelian lifted his patch and winked with a twinkling eye I thought I'd never seen before, and said to his brother, "Beware of *this* one, Sarkis. He will go places."

Then he drove north toward Fresno.

GERALD W. HASLAM calls himself "an American mongrel" because of his mixed ethnic background. "Mal de Ojo," from *Condor Dreams and Other Fictions* (1994) dances between sense and nonsense as it explores how a mixed Mexican-Anglo boy tries to adjust to life with his grand-mother. Among his other books are *That Constant Coyote, Coming of Age in California,* and the multi-award-winning *The Great Central Valley: California's Heartland* (with photographers Robert Dawson and Stephen Johnson).

"They also were told to burn incense in front of the family Buddhist shrine each day to ensure Santa's granting their wish."

PAPA'S HOLIDAY SPIRIT

JEANNE WAKATSUKI HOUSTON

When my family gets together for reunions and holidays, a great part of the time is spent "talking stories." We like to reminisce about the past—the good times and the hard times. Inevitably, the communal memories center on Papa—his comic, sometimes heroic, but always flamboyant flair for life. Not a holiday passes that Papa's presence is not conjured up with "Remember when . . ."

One reminiscence of my older brothers and sisters deals with Papa and his idea about Santa Claus. Two weeks before Christmas they were instructed to write Santa and request one gift. They did this with fervent trust and belief in the white-bearded and seemingly jolly old man they had seen pictures of. They also were told to burn incense in front of the family Buddhist shrine each day to ensure Santa's granting their wish. Of course, he always did. But with such a clamor!

At exactly midnight on Christmas Eve, Santa would arrive. My brothers and sisters hid under the bed. They were terrified by the howling, the banging of pots and pans, the firecrackers exploding and sirens wailing! As if possessed by a poltergeist or shaken by an earthquake, the house trembled!

My brothers and sisters shivered under the bed, wondering about this benevolent fat man who laughed "Ho-ho!" and crashed around their house like a demon.

After the din subsided, Papa came upstairs and ushered them into the living room to see what Santa had left. "We always expected to see our house reduced to total shambles," my oldest sister, Eleanor, recalls, "but, no matter how poor we were, our one gift was always under the tree, unwrapped and carefully displayed, and everything was miraculously in order."

Papa was a young father in his thirties then, ardently participating in the great American festival of Christmas. His children were Americans, after all, and should know the country's cultural celebrations. It didn't matter that he lent his own cultural interpretations and added a few dramatic effects. As far as he was concerned, the pandemonium of the Fourth of July and New Year's Eve was an appropriate embellishment for Santa's visit to our house.

My memories of Christmas and Papa do not include Santa Claus. By the time I was born, nine children had preceded me, and I'm sure his enthusiasm for the yuletide extravaganza had long since waned. As far as rituals were concerned, his focus had shifted to New Year's Eve. Papa insisted everyone stay home and help Mama prepare "shogatsu," the Japanese feast for New Year's Day. By midnight, all the food had to have been cooked and the house thoroughly cleaned. Not a crumb or speck of dust could be seen; if we overlooked any, that meant our house would be dirty all the coming year.

"Purify," Papa said. He always took a bath at midnight and told us he was cleansing himself of the past year's bad karma. He said it was his yearly "confessional," the washing away of his sins.

But the memory I cherish about Papa and the holidays is one that reminds me of the generous, compassionate man he was. When I was six years old, we lived in Ocean Park, near Venice in Southern California. Our house was one block from the beach. The wide cement walkway that still separates the sand from the buildings served then as the gathering place for children, chess players, organ-grinders, and vacationing city folk from Los Angeles. Today, it hosts the unending promenade of roller skaters, bicyclists, break dancers, boa constrictor fanciers, and would-be celebrities.

One Christmas Day, my family sat at our big round table in the dining room, enjoying a traditional turkey dinner. Meals were always boisterous. That day was no different. Delicious smells wafted from the kitchen, and clanking knives and forks and clicking chopsticks were comforting background to loud laughter and talk. Suddenly, it became silent. Alarmed by this absence of noise, I looked up to see a strange man standing in our dining room. Everyone else, already aware of this new presence, sat like stone statues, forks and chopsticks frozen in midair.

The man was unkempt and shabbily dressed. His unshaven face was pale. He was obviously a drifter from the thoroughfare along the beach. We were all wide-eyed with apprehension, wondering what was to be done. I remember feeling very sad in that cold, silent moment.

Then Papa jumped up and shouted, "Well, Mama, what are you waiting for!? Can't you see he's hungry? Give him food!" Mama and my sisters scrambled into the kitchen, and we made room for him at the table. When the plate of food arrived he gobbled it down soundlessly. Within minutes, the room was noisy again, and we continued our Christmas dinner, not paying much attention to our uninvited guest. After dessert, he stood up quietly and left without saying a word. Neither did we.

No one ever spoke of that incident until many years later when I told it at one of our "talk stories" family gatherings. "Remember when . . ." I began. Everyone did, and we agreed the real sustenance that Christmas Day was given not to the hungry man but to us.

JEANNE WAKATSUKI HOUSTON is a native of Southern California, where her father was a fisherman. During World War II, when Jeanne was a little girl, her family was confined to a so-called relocation camp at Manzanar, an experience she explored (with her husband and coauthor, James D. Houston) in the award-winning *Farewell to Manzanar* (1973). This mother of three is a noted freelance writer.

"Short, chubby, and strong, he had been a bantamweight, before the flower shop had come along to give him a living, during the Depression."

PEATO

RAFAEL ZEPEDA

Pablo, or "Peato," who was not really my grandfather, but my step-grandfather, was a short man, stocky, with a nose turned flat to the right side of his face. His hair was black and curly and thin in the back. He spoke, breathlessly most of the time, in low tones. "John," he said to me the first day I started working there, "here's a dollar. Go down to Tom's and get a sandwich and something to drink. Milk."

"Don't you want something?" I asked.

"No, it's Friday, and they don't have fish."

He was one Catholic who never broke the rules whether they were obsolete or not.

He was there in the shop before I got there, which was nine o'clock. He had already gone to the flower market in L.A., where he'd bought roses, stock, pompons, glads, daisies, mums, and the azaleas that sat in the window. It smelled of rotten flowers that morning, like a swamp. He asked me to dump the old flowers, save the ones that could be salvaged, dump the water from the tall cans and fill them with water, and put a couple of squirts of Purex into the water to keep the smell back.

An old woman came in. Her hat looked like something she had stolen from a gaucho—flat and black with a red ribbon as a band. She wore it on a tilt.

"Mr. 'Peato'," she said, for they always called him "Peato" though his name was Prieto. "I'd like a little flower to take to a friend."

"Yes, Miss Ferguson. What kind of flower would you like this week? We have some nice gardenias today. Big ones. Fresh. You like those."

"No," she said, "not gardenias today. My friend is having a party for me, another birthday, so I'd like to take her a nice bunch of violets. You have any violets?"

"Yes, Miss Ferguson. I'll get you a bunch and put a bow on it."

"Wonderful," she said. "A nice pink bow."

He opened the refrigerator and reached in and got the violets. I'd seen this happen the week before and wondered how many birthdays Miss Ferguson had.

She looked toward me with my bucket in my hand, and she smiled, then said, "Oh, it must be wonderful to work in a flower shop. To make people happy and smell all these beautiful flowers all day. You're lucky, you know."

"Yes," I said, as I filled a tin bucket and dumped in the Purex. "I guess so." I knew Pablo had been there seven days a week for so long that he smelled like the flower shop even when he was away from it. His clothes, his black shirt and pants, were permeated with the sweet odor of stock and roses, and his fingers were cut and punctured by the rose thorns he'd stripped off; a black stain was embedded under his nails, on his thumb and forefinger, in the fingerprints of his hands. Short, chubby, and strong, he had been a bantamweight, before the flower shop had come along to give him a living, during the Depression. The fights were something he loved, like his steel guitar that he kept in the case, on the table below the skylight. His business partner then, Ed Cauffey, had been a wrestler and a drinker, also an unlikely guy to be a florist.

One night I had come in after delivering twenty or so bouquets to hospitals, mortuaries, and churches all over town, and he was playing his steel guitar—not well, but still he could carry a tune. It lay flat and he moved the chromed bar across the strings with his right hand, picked the strings with his left hand and made the twanging sound that was "La Paloma," the Dove.

I stood in the doorway and listened to him play, saw that he loved the guitar he kept so clean, unlike himself, unlike the flower shop that even though he tried he could never keep clean. "Hey, Johnny," he said when he noticed me. "How long you been here?" He put down the chromed bar and walked toward his overstuffed chair.

"Not long," I said. "All the deliveries are out."

"Good. Good. Good. A lot of work tomorrow. A lot of work. You coming early tomorrow?"

"Yes, I'll come early. At eight."

He sat in the chair, then started to finger the arm where there was a large worn spot, the stuffing coming out. He closed his eyes, rubbed his nose that I always thought must have hurt, must have made that heavy breathing of his happen. "There's a good fight tonight. Eight o'clock. Art Aragon and some black guy. Can't remember his name. You like the fights, yeah?"

"Sure, I like the fights. They're good," I said. "How long you been playing the guitar?"

"Oh, that." He laughed. "I don't play. I just play around. A pretty long time, though, you know. Before I used to fight, in the Depression. Cauffey, my old partner, got it for me then. Swapped it for a bottle of whiskey. Yeah, old Cauffey." He leaned back, his black shirt open at the top, the front wet and stained from the flowers he'd pushed and shoved into pots and into wrapped pine needle plaques. His hands were tired and sore from the day's work. He opened them halfway, and with his palms he rested his forearms on the chair. He began to doze. His head bobbed backward. His head bobbed forward. His mouth opened, and his eyes fluttered until he was out, as if he had been knocked out by some recent bantamweight of the day, this flower shop and all its work, its demands of time. "Funerals. Weddings. Flowers for all Occasions" was painted on the sign in the window.

RAFAEL ZEPEDA teaches writing at California State University, Long Beach . . . his hometown. He is a poet and short story writer of mixed Anglo-Hispanic background. "Peato" is an excerpt from "Dirt," which appears in a collection of his stories titled *Horse Medicine* (1991). Zepeda has also published a variety of verse with colleague Gerald Locklin. In 1992 he won a National Endowment for the Arts Creative Writing Fellowship.

"As the only girl in the family, Mandy was terribly spoiled. She had her own room, lots of pretty clothes, a shiny red tricycle, and a big set of horse teeth."

COUSIN MANDY

MARY HELEN PONCE

My friends and I liked to ride bikes. Each afternoon, once our chores were done, we went bike riding up and down the dusty streets of our small town. Faces flushed, hair ribbons flying, we tore off, wanting to be the first to reach the corner. We rode homemade scooters, tricycles, and wagons, too. The wagons were of metal with four large wheels; they were used to haul firewood, and also food from the corner store. The scooters were made of wood. They were really crates with four wheels and a handle smack in the middle. They were fun to ride.

We borrowed tricycles from our younger brothers, who hated for us to use them. Hoping we would soon give back their bikes, they sat on the porch to wait while we rode the trikes back and forth, wrenching them from one side to the other.

It was hard for bigger kids to squeeze into the short seat. Our legs dragged on the dirt and our shoes scraped the rock-strewn street. It was hard not to tip over. Although the tricycles were great fun, my friends and I liked best the two-wheelers, even those that were old and rusty. We rode bikes with twisted spokes, patched seats, and worn tires. Sometimes, in exchange for a candy bar, our brothers let us take turns around the block while they watched us pull the tricycles to and fro.

My friend Anita and I spent hours daydreaming about bikes. We made believe we each had our *vichlas,* as the rowdy kids called bicycles. Anita, who could be terribly picky, wanted a red bike with a green leather seat and purple rims. Mine had to be apple-green with a wide black seat. I cared nothing about the rims, or tire size, only that my dream bike carry me back and forth across the street in record time, so I could beat the boys. Girls pretended to like paper dolls and jacks, but secretly they wanted *una bicicleta* all their own.

Neither Anita nor I owned a bike. Most families on our street bought bikes only for boys. Some of our *papas* could only afford bikes from the Goodwill. These were painted in bright colors: blue, red, green, and had brand new tires. The only girl I knew who owned a bike was my cousin Mandy.

Her real name was Amanda, a name too pretty for her, I often thought. She was the youngest in her family and terribly spoiled. Mandy had her own room, lots of pretty clothes, a shiny red tricycle, and a big set of horse teeth. Whenever we visited, my brother Alex and I begged to ride her pretty tricycle.

When first we arrived on a Sunday visit, Mandy acted friendly. She smiled as if to show off her horse teeth, then showed us her room. We sat on the floor while she dumped out the toy box at the foot of her bed. Out came balls, dolls, jacks, stuffed animals, and old candy wrappers. Mandy let us hold each toy for all of two minutes, then grabbed it from our hands, threw it back in the box, and slammed shut the lid. Once she almost caught my hand in the box. When done, Cousin Mandy marched us to the front porch, where sat the prettiest tricycle I had ever seen.

The bike shone apple-red in the warm sunshine. The huge front wheel came almost to my waist; it had two small wheels on each side. White rubber grips covered the chrome handlebars that extended from the base. The adjustable seat was black and moved up or down. On the back wheels was a step. Attached to the front wheel was a rubber horn that made a loud noise when squeezed. Next to that was a round dial with numbers. I thought Mandy's bike was the most beautiful thing in the world.

"This bike," Cousin Mandy told us as she smashed her hand on the seat, "is my very own. I got it for Christmas . . . and I say who rides it, see?" Alex and I, scared to death of the horse teeth, said nothing. We dared not make her angry. We wanted to ride the red bike.

When her parents were nearby Mandy let Alex and me take turns on the pretty bike. But first, as if afraid we might scratch its chrome, she guided the bike down the porch steps. Mandy took her time pushing the bike down the three steps. *Plunk, plunk, plunk.* One hand on the leather seat, the other on the handlebars, she guided the bike to the sidewalk. Mandy stopped to polish the seat, as Alex and I waited. We itched to get going.

"Hummmm, who should I let ride first?" Mandy liked to tease. "Who has a nickel?"

"Not me," I quickly answered.

"I got three pennies, and a marble," said Alex. He dug into his pants pocket, eager to start pedaling.

At first Alex rode the red tricycle on the sidewalk. He knew Mandy was watching. When he got to the corner, he tore off, wheels spinning. He rode back and forth, his dark eyes glowing, until Cousin Mandy screamed, "That's all you get, Alex. Remember, you only paid me three pennies."

When it was my turn I straightened my dress, then adjusted the seat, which had been lowered for Alex. I wiped my sweaty hands, smoothed my Shirley Temple curls, hitched up my socks, then clambered atop the bike. Cotton dress crunched to my waist, hands tight on the handlebars, I rode down the walk.

I dared not ride too fast or act reckless, or Mandy would say I was a showoff and make me get off. I pressed down on the pedals, then rode in a wide circle. Mostly, I waited for Mandy to go indoors so I could honk the horn.

Cousin Mandy had one bad habit. Each time Alex and I reached the corner, she made us jump off the bike and walk back to the house, then *she* got on—and rode away.

"It's my bike, see? I'm gonna ride it as long as I want." She sucked a Sugar Daddy, pulled up her socks, then, as Alex and I waited, spit on her patent leather shoes and rubbed the toes clean. Now she was ready. Black curls bobbing, large teeth shining, Mandy rode away in a cloud of dust.

At times, bored with riding round and round, Cousin Mandy backed up the tricycle, adjusted the handlebars, then rode towards us. She picked up speed as she got closer, then flew past between Alex and me, her knobby knees bumping first me, then Alex. Round and round she went, coming closer each time, as Alex and I, scared stiff, jumped out of her way, then ran off. When it was time to leave, Mandy came inside. She licked the candy bought with my brother's money, and said good-bye.

One time Mandy and her parents visited us. After she said hello, Cousin Mandy stomped to the room I shared with Alex. "Where's your toy box?" she demanded.

"We don't have one," Alex said, looking at his feet.

"That's 'cause you're poor," Mandy said smugly as she pulled up her pretty socks. "But we're not." She turned up her nose at Gita, my Raggedy Ann doll with red hair which our dog, Perro, liked to chew. Mandy walked to the window, then flopped on my lumpy bed. She seemed terribly bored.

Alex was the sweetest brother anyone could want. He wanted to make Mandy happy, so he showed her our tree house.

"Wanna climb it?"

"Well, I better not fall down, or . . ."

Mandy followed Alex up the wooden planks, then stopped in midair to rub the dirt off her patent leather shoes. We sat on planks nailed to the tree trunk and looked up at the blue sky. From here we could see the whole town: the church, school, and corner store. Alex and I threw rocks in the street and waved at our friends. Mandy acted bored until Alex mentioned our tire swing.

The swing, made by our *papa,* was an old tire with a long rope hanging on the side. It hung from a branch of my favorite eucalyptus tree.

Alex and I took turns helping our cousin crawl inside the tire. "I better not dirty my new dress," Mandy cried. She smoothed the velvet dress with lace cuffs. "And I better not scuff my brand-new shoes." When I started to protest, she said, "You don't care 'cause *your* shoes are old."

I stared down at my feet, at the school oxfords I polished once a week, right before church. I *liked* my shoes; they were all I had. When laced up they hugged my feet and during recess, kept me from falling. Still, Cousin Mandy's shoes with the little heel were so pretty!

Mandy waited while Alex crawled inside the black tire. He grabbed the rope with his small hands, then began to swing. Back and forth he went, dragging his feet across the dirt. Higher and higher went Alex. Even Mandy looked impressed. Suddenly, she yanked the rope—and pushed Alex out—then squeezed herself inside the tire. Scrawny arms dangling, long legs skimming the ground, she screamed at Alex: "Pull the rope. Harder, harder."

Alex pulled with all his might. His face was flushed and sweaty. Perro, never too far from Alex, began to bark. *Arf, arf, arf.* Faster and faster went Cousin Mandy, as I yanked on the rope. When she came near Alex her arms flailed out, as if to hit him. Back and forth she went, as Alex and I watched.

Just then Mandy began to scream: "Stop, stop the swing! I'm gonna be sick . . ."

We stopped . . . but not in time. Cousin Mandy, her dress dusty and wrinkled, crawled out of the tire. She clutched her hand to her stomach, went behind the eucalyptus tree, and threw up all over her patent leather shoes. Alex held his nose; I turned away.

Soon after, held up by her doting parents, Mandy came to say goodbye. The velvet dress looked and smelled awful; her shoes were dirty and scuffed. "I'm never gonna come here again," she hissed to Alex and me. "You're too poor! You don't have any toys. And your dumb swing makes me sick!"

True to her word, she never visited again. As we grew older our parents no longer drove the long distance to her house. But I never forgot Cousin Mandy—and the shiny red tricycle with the leather seat.

MARY HELEN PONCE, the mother of four, is the author of many revealing short stories about growing up as a Chicana. Some of her fiction was collected in *Taking Control* (1984). More recently, she published an autobiography, *Hoyt Street* (1993). She teaches at California State University, Northridge, and at UCLA.

"I am that generation of Chinese-Americans who fled the Chinatowns. The invisible breed. The shamed . . ."

A JUK-SING OPERA

GENNY LIM

I had this dream where I was inside a museum surrounded by ancient Chinese artifacts. The feeling of reverence and exaltation was great each time I discovered a precious object retrieved from memory or association. Silk garments with hand-embroidered dragons and phoenixes, porcelain cups, opium pipes, a hand-carved camphor chest with intricate motifs, jade and ivory carvings, vases once touched, possessed or seen in the past and long forgotten. Discovering an old rattan trunk, the type my uncle might have brought to Angel Island, I am moved to ecstasy and suddenly break into song.

The music that emerges from my mouth, however, fills me with amazement. I am singing Cantonese opera! It's as if I'm possessed by another being. My voice rises and falls in a familiar falsetto. The only time I have heard such virtuoso singing like this was as a little girl at the Great Star Theater, where the traveling operas came once a year. They, too, had to stay on Angel Island each time they came to tour. In fact, they entertained the detainees to alleviate their depression and boredom. The crowds in *Die-Fow*

(San Francisco) loved them so much they would shower them with fabulous collars made of dollar bills. Now I become their idol, singing like a Hung-Sung-Nui, the famous opera star, with every soul rapt in my hand's palm. My phrasing and timing are precise, my tone clear and shrill like a flute as my voice slides through a series of varying pitches on the same syllable, turning vocal cartwheels in steep-falling rhythmic cadences.

I awaken and the opera vanishes. The illusion of transcendence and self-mastery is suddenly gone. I'm still a tongue-tied *hu-ji nuey,* an American-born Chinese girl in San Francisco.

But I can still hear the opera echoing in my ears. Its lyrical melody lingers, leading me like the zigzagging line on a highway map to a destination unknown.

As the youngest of seven children, I often felt removed from any sense of a cultural past. As a second-generation American-born Chinese, I was often a living contradiction of dual values and identities. At home, my Chinese-ness gave way, much to my mother's sadness, to American-ness; and outside, my American-ness always belied my Chinese sensibility. If the twain theoretically never met, they certainly often collided for me.

As a little girl, I bristled with shame and outrage as I heard people call my father "Chinaman." Yet his erect, proud bearing never betrayed any anger or humiliation. And I now realize the alienation that pride cost him. Because of his need for the secure kinship of fellow villagers, Father never left Chinatown. He would not hear Mother's constant cry to leave the ghetto for the suburbs of the city. One of the very few places where he did take us was the Sacramento Delta.

In the old days it would take Pop about four hours to wind his way through the highways to the delta. Perhaps the trip took so long because of his growing confusion over the new freeways that kept springing up overnight. Our out-of-town trips trickled to about one a year, only for special clan occasions, like the Bomb Day celebration in Marysville, where a frenzy of overzealous young men vied for the coveted prizes that signified the appeasement of the goddess *Bok Kai,* thrown into a crowded square. Sometimes fights would erupt over the cylindrical, red-wrapped prizes, which contained a gold ring, and sometimes we would get jostled or stepped on. Once in the melee I cried in terror as I was knocked to the ground. Maybe *Bok Kai* could ward off floods, but she didn't seem effective against stampedes.

Father was part-owner of the Golden Lantern Restaurant in Sacramento. All I remember of the place is the golden lanterns strung from the ceiling, the green matchbooks with gold lanterns embossed on the cover, the steamy, bustling kitchen where we kids were not allowed, and the dark storeroom where we spent hours rolling around on a dolly and climbing up boxes stacked almost ceiling high. I enjoyed the summer trips to Sacramento, if only as a departure from the daily existence of Chinatown. Once we slept in an unair-conditioned hotel room and I could hear my brother and sister having a water fight in the bathtub next door as I tossed and turned in bed. Once we discovered an empty storefront and spent the morning impersonating mannequins, to the amusement of passersby.

The banquets were memorable. Unlike today's banquets, where people eat and run, they were all-day family affairs. Cases of Bireley's orange soda, sparkling cider, Seagrams 7, mounds of *gwa-chi* (melon seeds), candy kisses, coconut candy, were always on hand. In the screened-off area the men, and very often the women, gambled and talked loudly, among the din of clacking *mah-jongg* tiles, dominoes, and Cantonese opera blaring from the loudspeakers. One elderly woman passed water right in her chair, she was so engrossed in her game! The men liked to drink and make speeches. They toasted from table to table during the nine-course banquet, ignoring their wives' worried glances.

The Cantonese people that I knew were very different from the Chinese people I read about in newspapers or books. They did not resemble the fawning stereotypes I saw on television or in films. The Cantonese I had grown up with were vibrant, adventurous, passionate, courageous, proud, and fiercely loyal family men and women. The men were given to bouts of drinking and gambling, often as their sole escape from a lifestyle of virtual exile. The women embraced their rituals and superstitions as a talisman against harm, appeasing the gods with chicken and wine on Chinese New Year's Day, consulting soothsayers and oracles from yarrow stalks, and chanting to ward off evil spirits.

I am sitting in Mrs. Wong's living room in the town of Locke, which is near Sacramento, and am looking up at her wallful of memories—children, grandchildren, husband, young wife. . . . I am touched with sadness. I want to bring her oranges once a month, sit and chat with her about the size and brilliant color of her *gwa,* her infallible fishing technique, her expert knitting, which she proudly holds up for my inspection. A white vest for her only son, who lives in Sacramento with his family. I do not ask how often he comes because I know it is not often enough.

I become that son, sharing in his guilt. I am that generation of Chinese-Americans who fled the Chinatowns. The invisible breed. The shamed, who like the Jews bury the scars of the Diaspora; but unlike the Jews, we cannot escape our yellow skins behind masks of white.

She brings me an ice-cold can of 7-Up. I am not thirsty, but I graciously accept. It is safe here, better than the city. I think about my mother wandering like a frightened child in the darkness; my thoughtlessness had sent her unknowingly into the new underground metro-muni subway. The train never emerged from the tunnel, and she could not read the English signs. She could not even return to her departure point because the train had switched routes at the end of the line. Mother wandered the length of the city, looking for a familiar Chinese face, any face.

It does not matter that my mother and Mrs. Wong have been in this country a majority of their lives. Their lot as Chinese women has been circumscribed, preordained here as it was in China, except that now there was no need for bound feet. Like Mother, Mrs. Wong has never learned to speak English. Life in Locke and other American Chinatowns was self-sufficient, insular. You toiled in the fields, orchards, factories, sweatshops, and came home at night to your own teacup, bowl of rice, and four walls. There was a curtain that hid you from the outer world. . . .

"You hold his hand right now!" the white kindergarten teacher scolded as the children filed out in pairs for recess. How could I explain to her what the other Chinese children had told me—that skin color was transferable. If I held the Negro boy's hand, I too would turn as dark as a *see-you-guy* (soy-sauce chicken). Deep within, I sensed my attitude was perverse, yet I still spent the remainder of recess in the lavatory, scrubbing the ubiquitous mark of Cain, which the Mormon missionaries who came to Chinatown spoke about, from my palm.

I used to hide my lunches from the other kids because they laughed at my *joong* (sweet rice with a duck-egg yolk, pork and peanut filling, boiled into a glutinous lump wrapped in banana leaves), or they would wrinkle their noses in disgust at my greasy deep-fried Chinese New Year's dumplings and other such incriminating un-American concoctions. Being Chinese in America always seemed a liability to me until much later in my youth when I realized the lack of any identifying American culture.

Before Father died, I tried to convey to him the importance of reclaiming our Chinese-American history. My father, like so many of his first-generation cohorts, however, always felt that what history was lost was not worth retrieving. "What's the use?" he used to say with a helpless shrug. Years later, as I talked to an old man in Locke, I was to hear the same words repeated over and over. "*Mo-yoong, mo-yoong . . .*" he kept repeating bitterly. "It's no use, it's no use . . ." He tells me his family was slaughtered in the war (Sino-Japanese), and blinks back tears. "Nobody's left here," he says, gesturing around the crumbling wooden house with an age-peppered hand. "*Mo-yoong-ah . . .* And I'm too old."

I dreamt Father was alive. I nuzzled against him the way I did as a small child and felt his warmth. The hands that held me were smooth, gentle, unlike the tensed veins that stood out on the back of his hands and the tapered fingers that tapped nervous rhythms on tabletops, the calloused palms once swollen white with pus and sores from beating flames out of my hair and clothes when the sash of my dress caught in the open gas fireplace while I was thumbing through the pages of a Montgomery Ward catalog (my favorite pastime).

Like watching a fading dinosaur, I watched Father's strength give way to age. This handsome, worldly, natty *gum-san-hock,* this guest of the Gold Mountain with the impish grin, who once boasted he owned the first LaSalle in Chinatown; the Arthur Murray dance expert who could rhumba, swing, and out-fox-trot any *bok-guey* (white demon) since Fred Astaire; the droll Chinese Jack Benny who refused to age beyond his long-past thirty-nine years; the hot-tempered septuagenarian who bellowed Cantonese opera around the house and who once challenged a rude young clansman less than half his age to a fight for turning down the Cantonese music during a banquet—had become the inevitable victim of a dying breed.

The twinkle in his eyes disappeared into two cloudy cataracts and soon into two distant gray moons blinking behind Coke-bottle-thick lenses. I saw the once quick, reptilian grace slow to measured, halting steps intermittently punctuated by coughs and breathlessness. But most frightening of all, I saw him sleeping corpselike but still breathing in the winter before his death. My four-year-old daughter whispered as we peeked into his room, "Is *Gung-Gung* [grandfather] going to die?" I hushed her and quickly closed the door.

Father came to *Gum-San* three times in his lifetime. He came as a young boy with Grandfather. He returned at sixteen to China, then came back. It was on his third trip to China that he married Mother. He lived with her in *Chel-kai* for four and a half years before coming back to the States for the last time.

He always threatened that when I turned eighteen he was going to return to China. Then his duties as husband and father would have been fulfilled. Like many of his kinsmen, however, he saw the dream of retiring in wealth to their native villages destroyed by the Communist takeover in China.

It has taken me many years to reconcile my father's pain with my father's pride. I remember as a little girl holding my big Poppa's hand as we walked into his sewing shop on Powell and Vallejo. We were greeted by the hostile presence of a towering redheaded white lady. She stormed at him, "Mr. Lim, if you do not finish this lot by next Wednesday, I'm going to give the next shipment to another Chinaman. Is that clear?"

I remember how I waited with anxious anticipation for my fearless father to tell that ugly old white lady to shut up and then hit her. I remember how stunned and confused I was when my father did nothing; instead, head bowed, he answered under his breath, "OK, Ci-Ci."

I feel rage spilling into me as I think of how on that day Ci-Ci towered above us like a redhaired ghost, reducing my beautiful, shining, mythological father into an insignificant Chinaman.

That was twenty-five years ago. I have not had to make such compromises in my life, thanks to my father. His legacy of sweat and hard work has left me with a richer life and is still very much alive. It is the Cantonese opera. I hear it in my sleep, in my dreams. It awakens that part of me which lay buried deep along the Pacific route to America decades before I was born. I can sing it perfectly in my sleep. The Cantonese flows out of my lips like the Pearl River.

I might have been a diva in China. It used to frustrate me that the moment I awakened the language would be lost. Now I see the loss can be taken as a gain. The trick is to render the opera in English when I awake. In spite of what the critics and skeptics say, I know it can be done. It's like learning a whole new language. I rather like my *juk-sing* phrasing. Who says a hollow bamboo can't sing?

GENNY LIM is a playwright, poet, and performer who was raised in San Francisco. Her drama *Paper Angels* won the Villager Award for Best Play in 1982 and was televised nationally on American Playhouse in 1985. She is also coauthor of *Island: Poetry and History of Chinese Immigrants on Angel Island*.

NEW EXPERIENCE,
OLD WISDOM

"Aunt Geeta wore her hair in the neat bun that most middle-aged Indian ladies favored."

GROCERY SHOPPING WITH AUNT GEETA

CHITRA BANERJEE DIVAKARUNI

Aunt Geeta was fumbling with the catch of the seat belt even before the car came to a complete stop. And before I could switch off the engine, she had swung her door open and was standing in the parking lot of the grocery store in the quiet Sunnyvale neighborhood where I lived.

"I've always wanted to visit an American food shop!" she said, smoothing back wisps of gray hair and brushing out her sari, oblivious to the glances of the grocery clerk who was out gathering stray carts. "It seemed so interesting from your letters, so different from our Indian bazaars."

Aunt Geeta wore her hair in the neat bun that most middle-aged Indian ladies favored. Her hairstyle and her white cotton sari made her look so much like my mother had when I'd seen her last, waving good-bye to me at the Calcutta airport four years back, that a pang went through me. Like my mother, too, she had unbounded energy and curiosity. This was her first visit to America, and I'd already had a lot of fun sharing with her important aspects of American culture such as Egg McMuffins (being a staunch Hindu, she wouldn't eat a burger), *The*

Cosby Show ("Where *are* all those people?" she kept asking of the canned laughter), and the Versateller machine outside Bank of America ("You mean all you have to do is slide in that bit of plastic and punch in some numbers, and the money comes out, like magic? Why, that machine is smarter than a lot of people I know"). Now I was waiting to see how she would react to her first grocery store.

I wasn't disappointed.

"How huge it is!" exclaimed Aunt Geeta as she walked in. For a moment I saw the store through her eyes, shelves upon shelves crammed with brightly colored cans and bottles and packets stretching all the way to eternity.

"I can't believe how much food there is!" she was saying now. "Walls and walls of food. Why, what's in here could feed a thousand people! Not like Kesto's little store down the street from my flat in Calcutta. But where are all the people?"

The image of an open-air Indian bazaar flashed through my mind. Jostling crowds, the ground churned to mud by hundreds of trampling feet, the pungent smell of chilies and mint and molasses made from sugarcane. And the din! People bargaining at the tops of their voices or greeting friends shopping at another stall. Vendors shouting "fresh hilsa fish, caught just this morning," or "sweet melons, two for a rupee." Buses and cycle-rickshaws honking at sauntering pedestrians or at cows paused to chew on old vegetables thrown into the gutter. In contrast, this store in suburban Sunnyvale seemed sedate and placid, almost asleep. I explained that since it was 6:30 P.M. people were probably at home having dinner. But even during peak hours it was never crowded like Jogu Bazaar in Calcutta. There just weren't that many people, not even up in San Francisco.

"Dinner so early? Why, at home no one eats till eight or nine, not even the children! But the shopkeepers—where did *they* go?"

I pointed out the cashiers at the checkout stands.

"You mean you just put everything you want into the cart and take it up there and pay for it? As much as you want? No rations for rice or sugar, like we have? And they let you *touch* everything? Even the vegetables and fruits? Remember how back home Kalu the *sabji-wallah* would have a fit if anyone wanted to check his squash for freshness or his cauliflowers for green worms? . . . Hmm, eggplants. What's that? I see, it's the same as our *brinjals.* Sixty-nine cents each—can I really choose whichever one I like?"

I nodded, and after careful examination Aunt Geeta victoriously held up a huge purple eggplant for me to inspect. "This is the plumpest one, for sure, and see, when you tap it with your finger it doesn't make a hollow sound, like this other one. That means it's young and sweet, not so many seeds. Shall I roast it for you tonight?"

I agreed readily. My usual dinner consisted of salad and flavored yogurt, or a warmed-up can of soup, with maybe a frozen burrito or two thrown in on days I was really hungry. It seemed too much trouble to cook for myself, especially the delicate Indian recipes that required dozens of ingredients and had to be stirred for what seemed like hours over slow heat. Besides, Aunt Geeta was quite a cook, even better than my mother had been. Her roasted *brinjal,* baked in a mud oven until the skin was crisp and the insides melted on your tongue, was a legend among the family. I was confident she'd do a great job once I explained to her how my electric oven worked.

"Let's see now, what else do I need? . . . Oh, yes, onions and tomatoes and green chilies. Do you get green chilies here? Probably not. Too hot for the Americans, probably. My cousin Shefali who lives in Ohio says she has to make a special trip to the Indian grocery in Columbus to buy them. Takes her forty-five minutes! Can you imagine that! Forty-five minutes just for chilies! . . . How about coriander leaves? You probably don't get those either."

I steered her with some satisfaction to the jalapeño peppers and the cilantro, happy to be able to demonstrate California's superiority to the Midwest. I then explained that due to a large Mexican population in the area, we were lucky enough to find them in almost every grocery. Besides, the people of the Bay Area were fond of ethnic foods, and Indian cuisine was one of their favorites. There were over fifteen Indian restaurants just within driving distance of Sunnyvale.

"Are you serious? Are there really that many? Wait till I tell my friends in Calcutta! They'll be tickled to death to know that the *sahibs* are eating our food! Oh, here's the coriander leaf. . . . Mmm, nice and fresh. Here, smell!"

I held the pungent green bunch to my nose, remembering how my mother used to grow it from coriander seed in our backyard. And all those wonderful things she used to flavor with it—potato curries, lentils, Indian *pulao,* where it added color and taste to the mounds of rice. My favorite had always been a chutney where she used to grind the emerald-colored leaves with lemon juice, salt, and a pinch of sugar. We would eat it spread over potato *pakoras* on rainy evenings. Suddenly, after years, I felt terribly homesick as I thought of it. How much I'd left behind when I decided to move to America, how much I'd taken for granted, thinking it would remain there, unchanged, waiting for me. I wished now that I'd at least taken the trouble to learn the chutney recipe from my mother before I left India. Now, three years later, she was dead of a sudden brain tumor and I was left with the memory of monsoon skies weighed down with great black-bellied clouds, the sound of the rain mingling with my mother's voice telling a story, this same cilantro smell permeating her sari as she gathered me close for a hug.

"Tell you what," said Aunt Geeta, looking at me as though she could read my thoughts. "Let's buy another bunch of coriander leaves, and you can help me make some chutney—I'll teach you how, that way you can make it even after I go back. We'll fry some *pakoras* to go with it, and sit around talking, just like the old days. Won't that be fun?"

The cilantro leaves were cool against my face, like healing fingers. I laid them carefully in our shopping basket and turned to give Aunt Geeta a hug. "It'll be wonderful, Auntie!" I said, smiling, and together, arm in arm, we walked to the checkout stand.

Notes:

bazaar: open-air market

cilantro: leaves of coriander

pakoras: Indian appetizers made of vegetables dipped in batter

pulao: Indian fried rice

sabji-wallah: vegetable seller

sahib: foreigner (used for whites)

sari: Indian dress for women, made of six yards of cloth wrapped around the body

CHITRA BANERJEE DIVAKARUNI, whose roots are in India, lives and teaches in northern California. The publication of *the reason for nasturtiums* (1990) established her as an important poet. Of late, she has been producing verse exploring the experience of Americans of Indian extraction. She lives in Half Moon Bay, California.

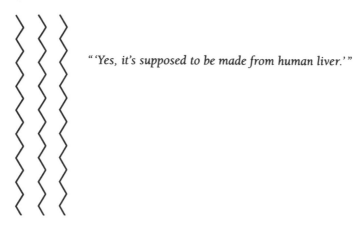

"'Yes, it's supposed to be made from human liver.'"

DRIED SNAKESKINS

HISAYE YAMAMOTO

As a child, you don't give such things a second thought. At least, I didn't. I remember once asking my mother about the *Aji-no-Moto.* She used to put a pinch of the white powder into almost every dish she cooked.

"Well, I don't really know," she said, "but it's rumored that it's ground from dried snakeskins."

Why dried snakeskins should improve the flavor of food or who first tried using them were questions that never occurred to me. Now that they occur to me, it turns out that it wasn't dried snakeskins at all—merely a chemical product called monosodium glutamate which almost any grocery store can sell you in tins labeled Accent or Zest.

Then there was this tall, smooth-faced, Japanese-speaking Korean vendor of rare and expensive medicines who came around once or twice a year. My mother used to buy several kinds of remedies from him: *Chosen-ninjin, jintan, kuma-no-i,* and *rokushingwan.*

The Korean carrots were small, pale, withered things which my mother would include in chicken broth whenever we children were convalescing from some illness or other. The *jintan,* which were tiny, silvery pills, like drops of mercury, were given us when we complained of headaches. They came in a charming little tin with a sliding, slotted cover which permitted removal of a pill without spillage. (I also liked the miniature spoons which came in *Aji-no-Moto* cans.) The *kuma-no-i,* for stomachaches, looked deceptively like a dried black fig, and effective though it might be, it was the bitterest-tasting single thing on the face of the earth. Even my father, I recall, shuddered when it was his turn to twist off a smidgen to swallow. The *rokushingwan* was a febrifuge and the most fascinating of the lot. Infinitesimal black pills, smaller than sesame seeds, they came sealed in black wooden urns about the size of a fingernail, in turn encased in tiny boxes covered with silky purple cloth. I don't remember taking any of those, but I must have, and there's where the horror lies. Unless my aunt is mistaken.

Well, in talking to my aunt not long ago about these medicines and later reading up a bit on them, I tracked them down to rather prosaic origins. All but the *rokushingwan.* My aunt remembered them very well. In fact, she uses them occasionally even today, in between operations and shots of penicillin.

It turned out that the *Chosen-ninjin* was ginseng, the Chinese herb known botanically as *Panax schinseng.* Ginseng is also known to North America, in the variety called *Panax quinquefolium.* My aunt has always been given to believe that this excellent restorative for generally run-down bodies grows only in the remote mountains of Korea; hence the exorbitant cost of it and *jintan,* for counteracting nausea, which is made from it. As for the *Kuma-no-i,* small wonder it was bitter, being the shrivelled gall bladder of a bear.

But I don't know about the *rokushingwan,* I don't know about it at all.

"What is that made of?" I asked my aunt.

"I don't know the real story," said my aunt.

"What story?"

"Well, it's just hearsay," said my aunt. "But, anyway, we were always told that Koreans and Chinese went about killing one another to obtain *rokushingwan.*"

"Killing one another?"

"Yes, it's supposed to be made from human liver."

"Human liver?"

"Yes. Not only that, but back in my own little village in Japan, when I was a child, there were rumors that two children had been murdered in the woods, and that their murders had been commissioned by mortally sick persons who hoped to get well by eating their livers."

Well, if one *had* to eat human liver, I guess that would be the best kind—the tender young liver of children. Just the same, I keep telling myself that my mother was wrong about the dried snakeskins.

HISAYE YAMAMOTO was born in Redondo Beach, California. When she was eighteen, her family was incarcerated with other Americans of Japanese descent in a so-called relocation camp. Yamamoto began writing for a camp newspaper, and soon her stories were appearing in major periodicals. Many were collected in her 1988 book *Seventeen Syllables and Other Stories.*

"The ranch house sat among alfalfa fields, at the foot of tall blue mountains cut by a waterfall like a bright ribbon."

THE WAY WEST

CLARK BROWN

When I was a little boy I lived in the East and lived well, though I did not know it. When you are young everything around you is normal, because you have nothing with which to compare it. So I thought everyone lived in a big house with a lawn and rose garden and playhouse, and had a father who wore a suit and tie and hat and rode the train to New York City, to an office like the one where on Thanksgiving I watched the Macy's Parade. And I supposed that all third-grade boys wore neckties in public school, because that's what we had to do.

Then one morning my mother called me into her bedroom. We were standing before a full-length mirror, so I could see us, as I will see us for the rest of my life.

"Your father is dead," she said, and burst into tears. Then I broke into tears and felt a terrible sickness.

That was the end of the big house with the lawn and rose garden. We sent some furniture ahead, and my mother, sister, cocker spaniel, and I got into the old Packard and drove to California, stopping in Montana to see my father's family. They lived in Missoula, but my grandfather had a ranch forty miles north, and there we drove, past the Indians' cone-shaped lodges and the shaggy buffalo on the reserve. The sky was high and clear and blazing and stayed like that all summer.

The ranch house sat among alfalfa fields, at the foot of tall blue mountains cut by a waterfall like a bright ribbon. It was a low, rough building with a screened porch and a rifle hanging on the wall. Nearby stood a foul-smelling shack swarming with flies. This was the toilet or "privy."

My grandfather was a heavy, gray-haired man who wore thick black suspenders and smoked cigars. Often he had many people at the ranch, but sometimes he took me there alone, feeling there were too many women in my life. Now and then he would puff his cigar and study me. I was the last male Brown, and he was wondering how I would turn out.

He took me around the ranch, showing me the murderous hog that would eat me alive if I fell into the muddy pen. He sent me into the smelly chickenhouse for eggs, and there among the droppings and dirty straw and feathers I produced much squawking and flapping and worried about getting pecked. He rented a sour-tempered little pinto horse called Calico, and I spent hours in the saddle, wearing my aunt's hat and boots and pretending to be a cowboy, but each time I slipped the bridle over Calico's head and worked the bit into her mouth, I was afraid she would bite me.

I was concerned about my hands, maybe because I had seen men whose fingers had been eaten by farm machinery, and because one day I was riding Calico with my wrist lying on the saddle horn, and the hired man told me real cowboys never held the horn. I said I wasn't "holding" it, just resting my arm. He said real cowboys never did that either, so then I refused to touch the horn except getting on or off.

Calico wasn't fooled and sometimes turned surly, no matter how hard I kicked her or whacked her with my aunt's quirt, but once when my grandfather saw this balkiness, he cursed her and picked up a rock the size of a cantaloupe and threw it, hitting her in the rump. She sprang forward and trotted smartly wherever I wished.

I loved riding the horse, and I loved the big maroon barn stuffed with hay. The cows would come clonking and clumping in, and the hired man would milk them, shooting streams through the air for the cat, who reared up and caught the milk in its mouth. I liked this too, and I liked climbing the mountain of hay, but one afternoon I ventured down the other side and faced a fiery-eyed bull the color of tar, with wide sharp horns. He stamped and snorted, and I clambered back in terror.

There were surprises like that on the ranch, and it wasn't elegant, like the candlelight and crystal at my mother's New York dinner parties. Sometimes my grandfather heated food by running cans under the hot water. Once the labels came off, and he gave stew to the dog and ate the dogfood himself. When he discovered his mistake, he insisted dogfood tasted better than canned stew.

All this was new to me, and it was new being trained and watched, which I was. It was about this time that I first heard the heavy words, "You're the man of the house now. Your mother depends on you."

I wasn't sure what this meant, but I understood that it involved doing and not doing certain things, like putting your hands under chickens and into the mouths of horses but not on saddle horns, and it involved pretending dogfood tasted fine. At times too, I saw, manhood required you to lose your temper—with a sulky horse, say—and it could leave you wounded, like the stumpy-fingered farm workers. But most of all, I realized, manhood meant that sooner or later you would come upon someone with fire in his eyes and hate in his heart. When that happened, you were to be very brave.

CLARK BROWN is a novelist, essayist and short-story writer who teaches at California State University, Chico. As this story recounts, he was not born in the West, but discovered it in his childhood, so his perspective offers unique insights. His work has appeared in many periodicals, and he won a Pushcart Prize in 1985 for "A Winter's Tale."

"Amazing, I think to myself. Amazing how much America and its people have given us."

STEPPING STONES IN AMERICA

BAO-TRAN TRUONG

When I was seven years old, my family and I first arrived in America. We were people who had lost our land and were searching for freedom, and our pursuit of hopes and happiness.

That was eight years ago, when the only English words I knew were "yes" and "no." Now, I am able to write stories, term papers, poems, and speak the English language very well. Amazing, I think to myself. Amazing how much America and its people have given us. Now, both of my parents are working, and we are having a good life. My mom is an office assistant, and my dad is an engineer. I have one sister and one brother. My sister is a high school senior this year. Her current GPA is 4.0, and most of her classes are honors. My brother has excellent grades and, like many junior high students, he likes skateboarding. As for me, I am fifteen years old, and I can see myself maturing each year. I hope to top my current 3.67 GPA in my junior year. I know that if I work hard enough for it, I will succeed.

In spite of all these successes, it has not always been

that way for me. For many years, I tried to deflect my Vietnamese descent. It was only a few years ago that I was able to accept myself as a true Vietnamese girl. I remember those early years when I wanted an American name instead of my birth name, Bao-Tran. I wished that I had been born an American and that I could speak English as well as my American friends did. I hated myself for having almond-shaped eyes, black hair, and a small-frame body. All of these fragments of myself were the traces that belong to the Asian people.

During my elementary years, most of my friends were middle-class Americans. They wore brand-name clothes, while I shopped at a thrift store. They had houses, cars, money, family gatherings, popularity, and their homeland. All of these, I did not have. Whenever I saw a typical American family on a TV show, I wished that I was part of that family. It did not mean that I did not love my own family, but the family on TV seemed to be so perfect and civilized.

In the fall of 1984, I entered California Middle School. Years there have been precious to me. My seventh-grade year was a time when I learned to be more sociable with the people I had always wished to fit in with. The middle-class Americans gave me a warm welcome to their popularity group. The reason they liked me so much was that I was different from the people they grew up with. I was what they called "a weird but cute Vietnamese girl." They enjoyed listening to me talk because I had a funny accent, and I could not pronounce some of the English words correctly. Sometimes I would ask my friends what a certain word meant, and sometimes I would feel bad because the meaning was so obvious.

By the middle of my seventh-grade year, I had abandoned most of my Asian friends whom I had befriended in the sixth grade. I did not want to have any connection with my people anymore. I loved the fact that I was accepted by the American students. I came to act like my new friends, and I became a part of their lives. I copied their American teenager ways by "acting bad."

I thought that, to be a cool person, I was supposed to get bad grades, have a bad attitude, and be bad. Yes, I have tried all of these "bads," and I have to admit it was fun. Life is so much fun, I thought, when you are popular. I only wanted to be popular and have a lot of fun. I regret some of those times now. I regret that I did not want to be totally myself because I wanted so much to hide my Vietnamese heritage. I also regret a time when a friend of mine came up to me one day and asked, "You're Vietnamese?" I said, "Yes." She said, "You know, my dad was killed in the Vietnam War." What did I say? I said a quick, sympathetic "Sorry," and left it behind me.

That year was the year I experienced my dream of being popular, fitting in, being able to get to know a lot of people, and being like a normal teenager going through a teenager's phase. That year, I made "the seventh-grade girl of the month," and I was voted the "Most Hilarious Girl." Can you believe it? Being voted as the most hilarious girl, and I did not even know what the word "hilarious" meant!

My seventh-grade year had a great deal of meaning to me because I was accepted by the people I always wanted to be friends with. But in many ways, my eighth grade was more valuable to me because I began to see many qualities in myself. That year I began to find love and to respect myself. It all started in the beginning of the year when my friends became freshmen in high school, and I was still in junior high, not knowing a lot of people. Soon, I made many new American middle-class friends. This group of friends was more down-to-earth than those of the year before. They supported me and encouraged me to be myself. Most of those students were in tenth-grade-level core classes with me. Our core class contained a class of literature, English, and history. Some days, we would spend much of the time discussing our points of view of the world we live in. In that class the people and teachers respected my opinions, thoughts, and concerns. They had a way of communicating to me that it was all right for me to get good grades, have a good attitude, and be good.

During my freshman year in high school, my parents bought their first home. I had to leave all my friends at one school to attend another. My freshman year at the new school was a lonely year. I did not have a social life. I withdrew from the people and became a study-aholic. I considered myself a loner. Being a loner, I had a lot of spare time to myself. I began to study about the Vietnam War and its effect on American society.

What I read and found out about the Vietnam War was astonishing to me. I saw a picture of a marine soldier who stood tall and muscular, holding a machine gun, and smiling proudly. I turned the page, and it was the same man; only this time he was sitting in a wheelchair. He had lost both of his legs, and his spinal cord was broken. Other stories I have read were about how this country was split in half because of the war. Half of the Americans were for it, and the other half protested loudly against the war. Even to this day, people still demonstrate that they hated the Vietnam War with bumper stickers like "NO VIETNAM WAR IN CENTRAL AMERICA." When I see a bumper sticker such as this one, I feel ashamed of myself for being a Vietnamese.

On each Memorial Day, I felt like a criminal. I wanted to hide myself and my identity because I felt that my people and I were the cause of many Americans' deaths. I felt that if there were not a country called Vietnam, then maybe my friends' loved ones would not have died. So many Americans protested against the Vietnam War. They hated the many deaths of their people; how could they not hate me?

I continued to wonder about the Vietnam War and in my sophomore year I became involved in the speech tournament. With this new involvement, my speech teacher encouraged me to talk about Vietnam. After many speeches that I gave about Vietnam, I gradually began to accept my Vietnamese heritage. Now when I give speeches about my country, I realize that my country is beloved. I feel no shame, but rather I feel proud of myself for being a Vietnamese. When I wrote my speeches, I did a lot of research about my roots. It took me my whole sophomore year to acquire the bits and pieces of knowledge I needed to understand the Vietnam War. I became familiar with, but did not know, the whole history of the war and its effect on the American society.

With random knowledge, I did not fully understand the war or the conflict between the bureaucracies. Therefore, it never occurred to me that my people and I are the bystanders of the war. In the irony of the conflict, I gave a speech on the last day of my sophomore year about my feelings toward the war and the effect it had on me. To my surprise and bewilderment, my speech had a profound effect on my listeners, and some were in tears. When I saw tears and sympathy on my classmates' faces, a sudden revelation hit me. Americans were sympathetic toward me; they didn't hate me.

Now, I am always thankful and amazed at this country and its people. America and its people have given my family and my people a chance to pursue freedom, hope, and happiness. I believe that my family and I are very lucky to be living in America. Speaking for myself, this country has given me a chance to express my thoughts about a very difficult subject for both Americans and the Vietnamese. It also gave me a chance to pursue my hope of becoming a congresswoman someday. Without so many helping hands that have reached out to me in America, I could never have found the courage to reach inside of me.

When I looked back on the years of living in America, I can see myself maturing. It took a while for me to realize that in order for me to be happy with myself and my surroundings, I must express my thoughts and concerns freely. I know that deep inside of me, I was there, but I did not have the valor to believe in myself. Now I love my birth name because no one else I know has my name. When I spell B-A-O-T-R-A-N, I am spelling no other than myself!

BAO-TRAN TRUONG was a sixteen-year-old student at Elk Grove High School in California when she wrote "Stepping Stones in America." Her parents migrated from Vietnam in 1980, so she is part of the recent infusion of immigrant energy that has enlivened the West.

"She would do something awful, something embarrassing. She'd already been hinting that during the next eclipse we would slam pot lids together to scare the frog from swallowing the moon."

REPARATION CANDY

MAXINE HONG KINGSTON

We were working at the laundry when a delivery boy came from the Rexall drugstore around the corner. He had a pale blue box of pills, but nobody was sick. Reading the label we saw that it belonged to another Chinese family, Crazy Mary's family. "Not ours," said my father. He pointed out the name to the Delivery Ghost, who took the pills back. My mother muttered for an hour, and then her anger boiled over. "That ghost! That dead ghost! How dare he come to the wrong house?" She could not concentrate on her marking and pressing. "A mistake! Huh!" I was getting angry myself. She fumed. She made her press crash and hiss. "Revenge. We've got to avenge this wrong on our future, on our health, and on our lives. Nobody's going to sicken my children and get away with it." We brothers and sisters did not look at one another. She would do something awful, something embarrassing. She'd already been hinting that during the next eclipse we would slam pot lids together to scare the frog from swallowing the moon. (The word for "eclipse" is *frog-swallowing-the-moon*.) When we had not banged lids at the last eclipse and the shadow kept receding anyway, she'd said, "The villagers must be banging and clanging very loudly back home in China."

("On the other side of the world, they aren't having an eclipse, Mama. That's just a shadow the earth makes when it comes between the moon and the sun."

"You're always believing what those Ghost Teachers tell you. Look at the size of the jaws!")

"Aha!" she yelled. "You! The biggest." She was pointing at me. "You go to the drugstore."

"What do you want me to buy, Mother?" I said.

"Buy nothing. Don't bring one cent. Go and make them stop the curse."

"I don't want to go. I don't know how to do that. There are no such things as curses. They'll think I'm crazy."

"If you don't go, I'm holding you responsible for bringing a plague on this family."

"What am I supposed to do when I get there?" I said, sullen, trapped. "Do I say, 'Your delivery boy made a wrong delivery'?"

"They know he made a wrong delivery. I want you to make them rectify their crime."

I felt sick already. She'd make me swing stinky censers around the counter, at the druggist, at the customers. Throw dog blood on the druggist. I couldn't stand her plans.

"You get reparation candy," she said. "You say, 'You have tainted my house with sick medicine and must remove the curse with sweetness.' He'll understand."

"He didn't do it on purpose. And no, he won't, Mother. They don't understand stuff like that. I won't be able to say it right. He'll call us beggars."

"You just translate." She searched me to make sure I wasn't hiding any money. I was sneaky and bad enough to buy the candy and come back pretending it was a free gift.

"Mymotherseztagimmesomecandy," I said to the druggist. Be cute and small. No one hurts the cute and small.

"What? Speak up. Speak English," he said, big in his white druggist coat.

"Tatatagimme somecandy."

The druggist leaned way over the counter and frowned. "Some free candy," I said. "Sample candy."

"We don't give sample candy, young lady," he said.

"My mother said you have to give us candy. She said that is the way the Chinese do it."

"What?"

"That is the way the Chinese do it."

"Do what?"

"Do things." I felt the weight and immensity of things impossible to explain to the druggist.

"Can I give you some money?" he asked.

"No, we want candy."

He reached into a jar and gave me a handful of lollipops. He gave us candy all year round, year after year, every time we went into the drugstore. When different druggists or clerks waited on us, they also gave us candy. They had talked us over. They gave us Halloween candy in December, Christmas candy around Valentine's day, candy hearts at Easter, and Easter eggs at Halloween. "See?" said our mother. "They understand. You kids just aren't very brave." But I knew they did not understand. They thought we were beggars without a home who lived in back of the laundry. They felt sorry for us. I did not eat their candy. I did not go inside the drugstore or walk past it unless my parents forced me to. Whenever we had a prescription filled, the druggist put candy in the medicine bag. This is what Chinese druggists normally do, except they give raisins. My mother thought she taught the Druggist Ghosts a lesson in good manners (which is the same word as "traditions").

MAXINE HONG KINGSTON, a native of Stockton, California, is conceded to be a major American writer. In *The Woman Warrior* (1976), from which the preceding story is excerpted, she reveals (among many other things) the clash between Chinese parents and Chinese-American children. Hong Kingston's portraits of Chinese life in America do not dwell on generalizations about Chinatown but instead examine the experiences of individuals, which can be extrapolated by readers. She has remained equally original in the two volumes of her work that have followed *The Woman Warrior*—*China Men* (1980) and *Tripmaster Monkey: His Fake Book* (1990).

URBAN ENCOUNTERS

"I'm thinking particularly of an Okie kid who yelled that we were dirty Mexicans. Perhaps so, but why bring it up?"

BEING MEAN

GARY SOTO

We were terrible kids, I think. My brother, sister, and I felt a general meanness begin to surface in our tiny souls while living on Braly Street, which was in the middle of industrial Fresno. Across the street was Coleman Pickles and on the right of us a junkyard that dealt in metals—aluminum, iron, sheet metal, and copper stripped from refrigerators. Down the street was Sun-Maid Raisin, where a concrete tower rose above the scraggly sycamores that lined Braly Street. Many of our family members worked at Sun-Maid: Grandfather and Grandmother, Father, three uncles, an aunt, and even a dog whose job was to accompany my grandfather, a security guard, on patrol. Then there was Challenge Milk, a printshop, and the 7-Up Bottling Company, where we stole sodas. Down the alley was a broom factory and Western Book Distributor, a place where our future stepfather worked at packing books into cardboard boxes, something he would do for fifteen years before the company left town for Oregon.

This was 1957. My brother, Rick, was six, I was five, and Debra was four. Although we looked healthy, clean in the morning, and polite as only Mexicans can be polite, we had a streak of orneriness that we imagined to be normal play. That summer—and the summer previous—we played with the Molinas, who lived down the alley from us right across from the broom factory and its brutal "whack" of straw being tied into brooms. There were eight children on the block, ranging from twelve down to one, so there was much to do: wrestle, eat raw bacon, jump from the couch, sword-fight with rolled-up newspapers, steal from neighbors, kick chickens, throw rocks at pass-cars. . . . While we played in the house, Mrs. Molina just watched us run around, a baby in her arms crying like a small piece of machinery turning at great speed. Now and then she would warn us with a smile, "Now you kids, you're going to hurt yourselves." We ignored her and went on pushing one another from an opened window, yelling wildly when we hit the ground that, in our imagination, was a rough sea of snub-nosed sharks ready to snack on our skinny legs.

What we learned from the Molinas was how to have fun, and what we taught them was how to fight. It seemed that Sotos were inherently violent. I remember, for instance, watching my aunts go at one another in my grandmother's backyard, while the men looked on with beers in their hands and mumbled to one another, perhaps noting the beauty of a right jab or a left uppercut. Another time the police arrived late at night in search of our Uncle Leonard, who had gotten into a fight at a neighborhood bar. Shortly thereafter, I recall driving with my mother to see him at what she said was a "soldier's camp." She had a sack of goods with her, and after speaking softly to a uniformed man we were permitted to enter. It was lunchtime and he sat on a felled log laughing with other men. When he saw us coming, he laughed even harder.

In turn, I was edged with meanness; and more often than not the object of my attacks was Rick. If upset, I chased him with rocks, pans, a hammer, whatever lay around in the yard. Once, when he kicked over a row of beans I had planted, I chased him down the alley with a bottle until, in range, I hurled it at him. The bottle hit him in the thigh and, to my surprise, his leg showered open with blood. Screaming, his mouth open wide enough to saucer a hat inside, he hobbled home while I stood there, only slightly worried at the seriousness of his wound and the spanking that would follow. I shouted that he had better never kick over my beans. And he didn't.

I was also hurt by others who were equally as mean. I'm thinking particularly of an Okie kid who yelled that we were dirty Mexicans. Perhaps so, but why bring it up? I looked at my feet and was embarrassed, then mad. With a bottle I approached him slowly in spite of my brother's warnings that the kid was bigger and older. When I threw the bottle and missed, he swung his stick and my nose exploded blood for several feet. Frightened, though not crying, I ran home, with Rick and Debra following behind, and dabbed at my face with toilet paper, poked Mercurochrome at the bubbling gash, and then lay on the couch, swallowing blood as I slowly grew faint and sleepy. Rick and Debra stayed with me for a while, then got up to go outside to play.

Rick and I and the Molinas all enjoyed looking for trouble and often went to extremes to try to get into fights. One day we found ourselves staring at some new kids on the street—three of them about our age— and when they looked over their picket fence to see who we were, I thought one of them sneered, so I called him a name. They cussed at us, and that provocation was enough to send Rick to beat on one of them. Rick entered their yard and was swiftly caught in a whirlwind of punches. Furious as a bee, I ran to fight the kid who had humbled my bigger brother, but was punched in the stomach, which knocked the breath out of me so I couldn't tell anyone how much it had hurt. The Molinas grew scared and took off, while Rick and I, slightly roughed up but sure that we had the guts to give them a good working-over, walked slowly home trying to figure out how to do it. A small flame lit my brain, and I suggested that we stuff a couple of cats into potato sacks and beat the kids with them. An even smaller light flared in my brother's brain. "Yeah, that'll get them," he said, happy that we were going to get even. We called to our cat, Boots, and found another unfortunate cat that was strolling nonchalantly down our alley. I called "kittykittykitty," and it came, purring. I carried it back to our yard where Rick had already stuffed Boots into a sack, which was bumping about on the ground. Seeing this, the cat stiffened in my arms and I had trouble working it into the sack, for it had spread its feet and opened its claws. But once inside, the cat grew calm, resigning itself to fate, and meowed only once or twice. For good measure I threw a bottle into my sack, and the two of us—or, to be fair, the four of us—went down the alley in search of the new kids.

We looked for them, even calling them names at their back porch, but they failed to show themselves. Rick and I agreed that they were scared, so in a way we were victors. Being mean, we kicked over their garbage cans and ran home, where we fought one another with the sacks, the cats all along whining and screaming to get out.

Perhaps the most enjoyable summer day was when Rick, Debra, and I decided to burn down our house. Earlier in the summer we had watched a television program on fire prevention at our grandmother's house, only three houses down from us on Sarah Street. The three of us sat transfixed in front of the gray light of our family's first TV. We sat on the couch with a bowl of grapes, and when the program ended the bowl was still in Rick's lap, untouched. TV was that powerful.

Just after that program Rick and I set fire to our first box, in which we imagined were many people scurrying to get out. We hovered over the fire, and our eyes grew wild. Later, we got very good at burning shoe boxes. We crayoned windows, cut doors on the sides, and dropped ants into the boxes, imagining they were people wanting very badly to live. Once the fire got going, I wailed like a siren and Rick flicked water from a coffee can at the building leaping with flames. More often than not, it burned to ash and the ants shriveled to nothing—though a few would limp away, wiser by vision of death.

But we grew bored with the shoe boxes. We wanted something more exciting and daring, so Rick suggested that we brighten our lives with a house fire. "Yeah," Debra and I cried, jumping up and down, and proceeded to toss crumpled newspaper behind the doors, under the table, and in the middle of the living room. Rick struck a match, and we stood back laughing as the flames jumped wildly about and the newspaper collapsed into parachutes of ash that floated to the ceiling. Once the fire got started we dragged in the garden hose and sprayed the house, the three of us laughing for the love of good times. We were in a frenzy to build fires and put them out with the hose. I looked at Rick and his eyes were wide with pleasure, his crazed laughter like the mad scientists of the movies we would see in the coming years. Debra was bouncing up and down on the couch, a toy baby in her arms, and she was smiling her tiny teeth at the fire. I ran outside flapping my arms because I wanted to also burn the chinaberry that stood near our bedroom window. Just as I was ready to set a match to a balled newspaper I intended to hurl into the branches, our grandmother came walking slowly down the alley to check on us. (It was her responsibility to watch us during the day because our father was working at Sun-Maid Raisin and our mother was peeling potatoes at Reddi-Spud.) Grandma stopped at the gate and stared at me as if she knew what we were up to, and I stared back so I could make a quick break if she should lunge at me. Finally she asked, "How are you, honey?" I stared at my dirty legs, then up to her: "OK. I'm just playing." With the balled newspaper in my hand, I pointed to the house and told her that Rick and Debra were inside coloring. She said to behave myself, gave me a stick of gum, and started back to her house.

When I went back inside Rick and Debra were playing war with cherry tomatoes. Debra was behind the table on which the telephone rested, while Rick crouched behind a chair making the sounds of bombs falling.

"Rick," I called because I wanted to tell him that Grandma had come to see how we were doing, but he threw a tomato and it splashed my T-shirt like a bullet wound. I feigned being shot and fell to the floor. He rolled from behind the chair to hide behind a door. "Are you dead?" he asked. I lifted my head and responded: "Only a little bit."

Laughing, we hurled tomatoes at one another, and some of them hit their mark—an ear, a shoulder, a grinning face—while others skidded across the floor or became pasted to the wall. "You Jap," Debra screamed as she cocked her hand to throw, to which I screamed, "You damn German!" We fought until the tomatoes were gone. Breathing hard, we looked at the mess we had created, and then at each other, slightly concerned at what it might mean. Rick and I tried to clean up with a broom while Debra lay exhausted on the couch, thumb in her mouth and making a smacking sound. I don't recall falling asleep, but that's what happened, because I awoke later to Rick crying in the kitchen. Our mother had come home to an ash-darkened living room, a puddled kitchen, and tomato-stained walls. She yelled and spanked Rick, after which she dragged him to the stove, where she heated a fork over a burner and threatened to burn his wrists. "Now are you going to play with fire?" she screamed. I peeked into the kitchen, and her mouth puckered into a dried fruit as Rick cried that she was hurting him, that he was sorry, that he would never do it again. Tears leaped from his face as he tried to wiggle free. She threw the fork into the sink, then let him go. She turned to me and yelled: "And you too, *Chango!*" She started after me, but I ran out the front door into the alley, where I hid behind a stack of boards. I stayed there until my breathing calmed and my fear disappeared like an ash picked up by the wind. I got up and, knowing that I couldn't return home immediately, I went to the Molinas'. Just as I turned into their yard I caught sight of two of them climbing, hand over hand, along the telephone wires that stretched from above the back porch to the pole itself. A few of the younger Molinas looked on from an opened window, readying for their turn, as the radio blared behind them. I threw a rock at the two hanging from the wires, and they laughed that I missed. The other kids laughed. Their mother, with a baby in her arms, came out to the back porch, laughed, and told us God was watching and for us to behave ourselves.

GARY SOTO is among the most prolific and most honored writers of his generation. A native of Fresno, California, he established himself as a major poet with the publication of *The Elements of San Joaquin* in 1976. He has since, with the publication of collections such as *Living Up the Street* (1985) and *Baseball in April* (1990), become a landmark writer of fiction for younger readers. He also edited *California Childhood* (1988), an acknowledged regional classic.

"The boy was maybe ten, his skin like ebony velvet, with eyes that looked large and lost in a small, peaceful face, long-lashed and gentle obsidian."

ANIMAL RIGHTS . . .

JESS MOWRY

"Organizers in the Bay Area joined today in voicing support of an activist group claiming responsibility for vandalizing property in Santa Cruz County. The office and adjoining structure of a small business were ransacked, files were destroyed, and a bloodlike substance was splashed over walls and floors. According to a spokesperson for the activists, animals, primarily white rabbits, rats, and mice, were being raised on the premises for the purpose of laboratory experimentation. Cages were destroyed and all animals removed. The spokesperson refused to disclose where the animals were taken, saying only 'to a place of refuge and safety.' The spokesperson declined further comment, adding only, 'Animals have no one to speak up for them and their welfare should be the concern of every caring human being.' Authorities are still investigating. In local news, last night's drive-by shooting of an East Oakland youth . . ."

The boy stared at the TV screen, not hearing much more than the soothing cadence of the white lady's voice, or seeing anything but shifting colors. Dimly, he remembered his mom telling him something . . . a long time ago . . .

about *in one ear and out the other.* That was cool. Nothing stayed inside long enough to hurt.

The boy sat small, deep in the big old couch. It was covered in worn-out red velvet, but enough of the nap remained to feel soft on his body. There were no sharp angles to hurt him. He wore only jeans, faded 501's that were a little too small, so three of the buttons were open. They too were soft against his skin. The open buttons kept them from pinching. That was cool. Nothing hurt, and they were probably better than what he'd been wearing before . . .

Before what?

In one ear and out the other.

The TV voices droned on and the pretty colors shifted. If the boy thought hard enough he might remember that this was the early-morning news. Soon there would be cartoons. He didn't know how long he'd been watching the screen; all night, weeks . . . or years. It didn't matter. He drifted at peace in softness and warmth. If he concentrated he might have remembered more, but nothing hurt, so there was no reason to remember.

The boy was maybe ten, his skin like ebony velvet, with eyes that looked large and lost in a small, peaceful face, long-lashed and gentle obsidian. His body was just beginning to take on the puppy-look of major growing. He was thin. Small, tight muscles had started to define chest and arms but now seemed slack and fading as if no longer needed. His hair was bushy and wild, but clean, and scented with lice shampoo. Sometimes he was given a bath. Since when, he couldn't remember, but it didn't matter. Here he was, and nothing hurt.

There were cartoons. The *Teenage Mutant Ninja Turtles.* Vaguely he re-called it being a cool show that he liked. But now he couldn't remember their names.

The man's voice came from over his shoulder. "Boy! You got to go?"

The boy considered the words. What did they mean? He half turned his head toward the voice, but then forgot why. It didn't seem important.

"Shit!" said the voice. Then, "Irene! Get his ass to the bathroom fore he go an mess himself again!"

The boy didn't like the voice when it sounded that way. Maybe it reminded him of something? The woman came . . . Irene . . . and took his hand. It was a surprise to discover he could stand . . . that his legs held him up even though he walked on clouds. It was a surprise to find he *could* walk—to see his very own bare feet way down on carpet and then cross faded green linoleum one step at a time. Green like grass. He hadn't walked on much grass in his life. Even the linoleum felt soft. Linoleum grass. A new idea. The woman . . . Irene . . . set him on the toilet. He wondered if that should piss him off. After all, he wasn't a goddamn baby, and boys stood on their own two feet to piss. But that didn't seem to matter to the woman. Maybe she just wanted to be safe? He supposed he should do something, but seemed to have forgotten what it was. He was aware of the woman's hands, soft and warm on his bare shoulders, holding him. Her voice was carelessly gentle. "C'mon, boy, do somethin for moma fore you go noddin again."

The boy had a name, but he couldn't remember it. The woman . . . Irene . . . wasn't really his mother. Maybe he did do something in the toilet because he found he was standing on his own special feet once more, and the woman was buttoning his jeans. All but the top three. She led him back to the couch. There were more cartoons, but he wasn't sure what they were about. The old velvet was soft, but it seemed important to remember his name. Why?

The man's voice: "For chrissake, feed him, Irene! Saturday busy as hell . . . be goddamn 'barrassin' he die on us!" Laughter.

No, Irene wasn't really his mother. But mostly she was kinder than his mother had been. Even the man was kind in his way, though not as gentle-voiced anymore as when he'd picked the boy up in his big new car and brought him here. Wherever *here* was. It didn't matter. Here was a lot better than *there*. Here was warm and soft and nothing hurt.

Except . . .

The boy wasn't sure. Not yet. But he almost remembered.

A spoonful of color appeared under his small snub nose. Lucky Charms. Marshmallow shapes. Pretty. A spoonful of sweetness fed to him. He concentrated on not choking. Milk dribbled down his chin and chest. The woman clucked her tongue gently, the way his mother had done long ago. A soft cloth cleaned him up. Good as new. When had his mother been so kind? A long time before he'd come home from school to find the apartment empty? He was starting to remember. The Lucky Charms were sweet and crunchy, and the marshmallows melted to warm syrupy goo in his mouth. The woman was gentle as she fed him, waiting until he remembered to swallow, sometimes reminding him to. Did she love him? Most times she was kind . . . except when he messed himself like a goddamn baby. Or choked. Or forgot what to do on the toilet. Then she would shake him. Sometimes she'd shake him for no reason he could figure, but she never hit him. Even the man was kind in his way . . . he didn't want him to die.

The cartoons were almost making sense now. If he blinked his eyes and thought mega-hard he could remember things . . . fog drifting through the night streets, following him. Streetlamps haloed, cold, wet, and lonely. He shivered. It hurt to remember.

A knock on the door. Men-voices, mostly the man. He had a name . . . a street name . . . but the boy couldn't remember it. Yet. Maybe if he could remember his own name it would help? If he concentrated with all his might he could just understand the men's words . . .

"I tellin' ya, Jack, be prime product I got here."

"Yeah? An' how I know that, man? Could be death in a sandwich. Don't know you from nobody. Your price be the only thing I *know* prime, for a fact!"

The boy looked down at his arm. Sometimes it hurt. Things weren't supposed to hurt. It said on TV that it shouldn't hurt to be a kid. The man-voices, rising and falling, reminded him of that.

"Shit, man! You got to take nuthin on faith! Not from me. Come along here an' check this out. Right from the bag, see? You watchin?"

The boy stirred. The TV screen blurred. His arm hurt again and he began to remember. His name! Almost, he had it!

Man-shapes standing over him. Tenseness in the air. Smells of suspicion. Men-voices again. "Yo! Check this out. My own son here! Boy I love. Word up!"

The pain of the needle, sharp in his arm. Man-laughter. "Yo! He look like he dying to you, man? Hell, watch him long's you like."

More laughter. The voices fading . . . fading like the pain until nothing hurt anymore. All was softness and warmth, and sometimes even a gentle touch.

So why, the boy wondered, was he crying?

JESS MOWRY writes of the harsh urban world of his native Oakland, California, where children often must grow up fast . . . or not grow up at all. In July of 1988, Mowry bought a used typewriter and launched a writing career, with many of his stories based on his experiences as a counselor in Oakland. The publication of his first collection of stories, *Rats in the Trees,* in 1990 established him as a unique, powerful voice in modern fiction.

"My father would teach me how his medical instruments were used, or he would show me to his patients. I felt so close to him. However, since we came to this country, my relationship with my father has changed."

BOWLING TO FIND A LOST FATHER

MEE HER

We all held our breath as the ball slowly rolled down the alley. Then, just as it was about to hit the pins, it dropped into the gutter. Ahhh . . . We sighed in disappointment. My father slowly turned toward us. His eyes sparkled like those of a little boy, and a big smile was printed on his face. Then he joyfully chuckled as he walked to his seat. I never thought my father would enjoy playing with us. In fact, I never thought he'd enjoy fun. But on that evening when I taught him how to bowl, I did more than teach him how to hit pins. I had taken the first step toward bridging a gap which had been created between him and his children.

My father had never played with us. I guess that came with his Hmong orientation in valuing hard work. He told us that play was a waste of meaningful time which could be better used for productivity.

If we were still living in Laos where children don't have to go to school and all they do is work in the field with parents, my father's orientation would be the ideal. There, children would work hard on the farms, then, during break times, they would listen to parents tell stories of their own childhood. Parents also either would teach "music" lessons to their children with instruments that they created out of bamboo sticks or they would teach them how to blow and make music out of leaves. This kept the relationship between children and their parents close. But in this country, where everything is so sophisticated, parents don't know how to be close to their children.

I remembered my relationship with my father as a child. We went everywhere together. He took me to the hospital where he worked, to the fields, or to feed the stock on the farm. I remember the times my father took me to the hospital with him. My father would teach me how his medical instruments were used, or he would show me to his patients. I felt so close to him. However, since we came to this country, my relationship with my father has changed. He no longer knows how to be the father he used to be for us. He began to build walls around us by becoming so overly protective. He did not let us play outside or go out with our friends, using concepts of hard work to keep us at home like dutiful Hmong children. I felt emotionally distant from him. Somehow the gap seemed so great that neither he nor his children knew how to bridge it. As it turned out, I ignored our relationship altogether.

It wasn't until my third year in college that I decided to make my first move to recreate the relationship between my father and me. I had moved away from home when I started college. The time and distance made me miss the closeness that I used to have with him. I was beginning to see the need for closeness between my parents and the other children too. My father must have tried to keep the gap from getting larger when he became overly protective of us. It must have been frightening to live with children who did not live in the same world that he did. He couldn't play video games with them or couldn't understand ear-busting rock 'n' roll. He didn't even know how to play soccer or volleyball! And those were the things that his children did for enjoyment in this country.

Poor Dad. It was not his fault that he did not know how to be included in our lives. It was just that he didn't know how to get involved with his children. That was why my brothers and sisters and I decided to introduce my father to bowling.

I remember that day well when my brother, sisters, dad, and I went bowling. Dad was a little hesitant to come with us, but we all persuaded him. When we got to the bowling alley, we showed him how to hold the ball. Then we taught him how to throw the ball. It was a little bit foreign for me to be the one teaching my father, and I sensed that Father felt odd, too. But once he got the hang of it, he did well. He even made a couple of strikes!

I think it was much more than bowling that Father enjoyed. It was the emotional closeness that he felt with us which made him come back to bowl again. The next time we went bowling, he was teaching the younger children to bowl. As I watched him beam so happily with the kids, it occurred to me that this was the beginning of building a bridge across a long-created gap between Dad and his children. Another thought came to my mind too. I wondered why it had taken me so long to show my father how to bowl. Was I waiting for him to make the first move? Was I waiting for him to teach me instead? But how could he have done that when he didn't know how?

MEE HER's family came to the United States in the 1970s. They are Hmongs, and their epic escape from Laos—from the mountains, through the jungles, across the Mekong River, then the vast Pacific—more than rivals the hardships suffered by other, earlier American immigrants. She is a graduate student in psychology at California State University, Fresno.

" 'You know, it was hard today. The white man boss don't want to pay me what I make. I work fast. Faster than the other girls.' "

THE SEAMSTRESS

WANDA COLEMAN

Mama comes home tired from the sweatshop. She is so tired her body stoops—the weight of slaving on the double-needled power-sewing machine from 7:30 in the morning till 4:20 in the afternoon. So tired she can barely push open the door. So tired we are silenced by the impact of it on her face.

Mama comes home to the imperfect dinner almost ruined by the eleven-year-old anxious to please. To the petulant ten-year-old eager to play outside. To the five-year-old banging on his red fire engine. To the three-year-old crying for lack of attention.

Mama comes home to us so tired she must lay down awhile before she does anything.

So tired, baby, I could cry.

She goes into her room and collapses onto the bed. I watch from the hallway. She cries for a few minutes—a soft, plaintive whine. I go and set the table and serve the meal. I fix her a plate and take it to her on a tray. She is too tired to come to the table. *So tired, baby, I could die.*

We eat and my older brother and I do the dishes. Papa

has not come home. He calls. I take the phone to her. Her side of
the conversation is full of pain, anxiousness, and despair. So tired she
sounds.

But it's the beginning of the school term. And we need clothes for
school. We need. And I watch her rise.

"You know, it was hard today. The white man boss don't want to pay
me what I make. I work fast. Faster than the other girls. They get jeal-
ous of me. They try and slow me down. My floor lady is an evil witch.
She won't give me the good bundles. And she lets some girls take work
home to make extra money. But not me.

"I don't care. I'm so fast I do it all right there. And those Mexican
girls—they make me so angry. They all the time afraid. Won't speak
up for their rights. Take anything they'll give 'em. Even work for less
money, which weakens all our purses. We say, 'Hey—don't be afraid.' I
don't understand them Mexican girls."

She fills my ears with her days when she comes home from work. I
am the one she talks to. There is no one there to listen but me. Sometimes Papa is gone three or four days without word. And my brothers—
little boys too impatient for such stuff as what a woman's day is made
of. And her few friends—she talks to them by phone now and then.
She's too proud to tell them how hard it is for us. And since the hard
times, few friends come by.

She goes into the bathroom, washes her face in cold water and dries
her eyes. She goes into the front room and sits at the coffee table and
slowly, carefully, counts out the tickets which will determine her day's
wage. I help her make the tally by reading off the numbers aloud. Her
eyes are too tired to see them even with glasses. She marks them down
on a sheet of paper and adds them up. Satisfied, she gathers them up
and binds them with a rubber band.

I bring her fresh water from the kitchen. She drinks it in long, slow
swallows, then gets up slowly and goes over to her single-needle power
machine, sits and picks up the pieces that will become my new dress.
Within the hour I will try it on. She will pin up the hem and then sit in
front of the television and stitch it in. And tomorrow the girls at school
will again envy the one who always has new clothes.

But now I watch her back curve to the machine. She threads it with quick, dark cedar hands. She switches on the lights and the motor rumbles to life and then roars. *Zip zip zip*—the dress takes shape.

And this tired. I wonder as I watch her. What must it be like? And what makes her battle it so hard and never give in?

WANDA COLEMAN, an award-winning poet and fiction writer, was once a welfare mother, a dancer, a typist, and a waitress. Her books include *Mad Dog Black Lady* (1979), *Imagoes* (1983), and *Heavy Daughter Blues* (1987), which collects her poetry and prose from 1968 until 1986. Coleman is a fixture on contemporary Southern California's literary scene and a highly regarded performance reader.

"It was in the second grade . . . that I discovered if I drank pineapple juice for breakfast I would get sick at school and my mother would have to come and get me. She didn't like that."

SCHOOL DAYS

JOHN H. IRSFELD

For those of us whose lives revolve around schools, August is the real December. This is so because September marks for us the start of the new year, the start once again of school, one more chance to do it right.

The smell of buckram and chalk dust mingles with the faintly ammoniac odor of wet pants and children's sweat against old wood. The blackboards—which are green nowadays—have been recently painted, the wooden floors stripped and sanded and newly oiled; sometimes the desks have been stripped and sanded, too, excised of all but the deepest cuts of classes past: "Jack + Debbie," "J.R. '22'," "Class of '39." Olden times.

We enter the world of schools for the first time with trepidation or exuberance, shyly or rambunctiously. My sister Chris started down the street toward Cullen Grimes School, only to stop every few steps and turn around to see if my mother was still on the front porch making sure she got away okay. I don't remember my first day in school; I don't remember my first *year* in school. That's very psychological. The year was 1944.

I do remember second grade. Mrs. Ansley was my teacher. Her son, Gene, later an accountant in Chicago, was my age, but I don't think he was in her class. This was at William B. Travis School, Mineral Wells, Texas, grades one through seven. The State of Texas later added an extra year to make it eight like everywhere else.

It was in second grade that: there was a kid with a glass eye whom I envied even more than I did those who got to wear glasses; I spent several months on crutches because of an inflamed knee brought about by a bicycle accident; I smoked some of Mr. Tanner's cigarettes, which I stole out of his locker in the janitor's room and got spanked for taking; I entertained daily.

My favorite was the time I put a handkerchief over my tilted-up face and tried to determine when my classmates were lying and when they were telling the truth when they said Mrs. Ansley was back in the room. I bit twice on false alarms, but failed to bite the third time, only to have the handkerchief gently lifted away by Mrs. Ansley's own hand. It was that year that I discovered if I drank pineapple juice for breakfast I would get sick at school and my mother would have to come and get me. She didn't like that, and I quickly outgrew my allergic reaction.

Mrs. Bray taught third grade at William B. Travis. She was large-bosomed and had the best blackboard writing in school. You got cursive down pat in her room. She, personally, was formidable, yet I looked forward to my year there.

I didn't get to take third grade in Texas, however; in 1946 we moved to Washington, D.C.—really to a suburb in Virginia—and I spent third grade and most of the fourth in public schools of that sovereign entity. Of the coursework during that period I remember only Bacon's Rebellion—and that's all I remember about it, too, just the name.

But I do remember other great stuff, mostly from the fourth grade. Our school was in Falls Church, and the old building had been long outgrown, so a row of Quonset huts lined one side of the playground behind it. My class, which was half fourth grade and half fifth grade, was in the last hut of this row. First, second, and third graders were all closer to the main building, where the rest rooms were located. Sixth and seventh grades were in the main building. Eighth and ninth grades constituted middle school and were somewhere else altogether.

My teacher was Mrs. Lesansky, an unemployed marionettist who made it clear even to us children that she would have been happier at her real profession rather than being stuck with us. The only subject matter I recall at all is that we spent all of the year I was there—we left D.C. to return to the West in March of 1948—designing and sewing and otherwise assembling our own marionettes. We were going to put on a show at the end of school, and every class had to present a part. Our class was going to present a marionette version of the story of Prince Charming. I was doing Prince Charming, which seemed only right to me, since it was clear to me then and for some time afterward that I really *was* Prince Charming. But, as Woody Allen says, people change; love fades. Even, Irsfeld's corollary says, even for oneself.

But I went bad in the winter of '47. I don't know what came over me. It was probably nothing more than the manifestation of what kids feel when they become mature children at around ten or eleven years, just before puberty blitzes through like the Nazis through Poland and ruins them even further, if in a totally different way. I was awful.

One of my running buddies in another class, whose name is lost to me now, had an older brother who was a newspaper distributor. His job was to drive all over his area—which seemed to me to include a lot of downtown D.C. ten miles away, yet surely couldn't have—and dump out bundles of newspapers held together by baling wire. We would go to school all morning, building our marionettes, then eat lunch and tear around the playground afterwards for half an hour. Then, just as the bell sounded to summon us back to class, and all the proper, right-minded young people herded back inside, my buddy and I and whoever else we could commandeer would take off in the other direction, out the side gate of the playground and deep into civilian territory.

We would head into Falls Church proper, only a village then, and get some cigarettes—by then it was Lucky Strikes (red)—and go out behind the movie theater and smoke 'em up. Sometimes we would go into the dimestore on shoplifting forays. And then we would go to one of the newspaper drops and wait for the brother. When he came along, we'd load into the back of his panel truck and ride around for hours throwing bundles of *Washington Posts* out the rear doors, melting away thus by our own labor the comfort upon which we sat. For as the truck grew lighter, the ride grew rougher and the closer we sat to the splintery boards that floored the back of the truck.

Inside the Quonset huts were rows of schoolroom desks, of course, and cloakrooms at the back, and also potbellied iron stoves fueled with coal to keep our little fingers and toes from turning blue during what I, at least, after a lifetime spent way below the Mason-Dixon Line, thought was a very cold winter. I had a friend in my class, named Jack, although he was in the fifth grade half, which by right of seniority got to sit on the stove side of the room. I sat way across on the window side, which was the cold side, true, but which was also closer to the door and freedom.

My shoelaces came untied one day, which was not unusual since I had only just learned to tie them (a fact which I remind myself of periodically as one of the first evidences of what a slow learner I am). Somehow I got it in my head that if I could get Jack to tie my shoe-laces for me, I would, thus, assert my dominance over him, which was desirable, I guess, since he was a fifth grader and I only a measly fourth grader. I didn't think of any of this explanation at the time, of course. If I had been asked why, I'm sure I would have said, "I dunno." I had not yet learned the primary lesson of our public schools—our homes, our *culture!*—that "I dunno" is not an acceptable answer to any question.

So I sat down in Jack's chair. I said I had injured my back and could not bend over, so, at my request, he tied my shoes. Then he went to the back to the cloakroom for something. A moment later he came racing by me toward the front of the classroom, toward the potbellied stove. I was still seated sideways in his chair, my feet extended. I extended them only a fraction further as Jack came by. It was enough. He went sprawl-ing forward, straight into the red-hot stove, his hands out in front of him, of course, to break his fall, and subsequently, he burned himself. He was not burned badly, I hasten to say, but burned enough to cry. And burned enough to scare the hell out of Mrs. Lesansky, who thereupon, in her hysteria, ordered me to leave the room immediately and report to Mrs. Snodgrass, the principal, up in the main building. My God, I didn't *mean* for Jack to burn himself; I just wanted to see him fly.

As I headed toward the door across the room, Mrs. Lesansky said, "And you can forget about being Prince Charming, too!"

At the door itself I turned around, searching for a proper exit line, the last word, which I usually felt I had to have. "Oh, yeah?" I said. "Well . . . well, my dad's a major!"

I know, I *know.* It was a terrible line. But I was under great pressure. I was afraid of what I might have done to Jack. I was angry and hurt at losing Prince Charming. And I still had to face Mrs. Snodgrass.

It was, dare I say, with heavy heart that I trudged through the muddy playground up to the main building for my appointment with the principal, a woman so large, so forbidding, so . . . so *bosomy,* that she made poor Mrs. Bray look insignificant in comparison.

I dawdled. I dragged. I temporized.

I stopped at the water fountain just inside the back door of the main building. The basement floor opened fully out onto the playground, but only tiny basement windows showed over the lip of the front yard. I bent over to get a drink and the next thing I knew my face was smashed into the bottom of the fountain. I saw only a glimpse out of the corner of my eye of the free hand of the foul perpetrator of that deed and a forearm that had a ballpoint-pen tattoo drawn on it, of a skull with crossed bones beneath it, like the Nazi S.S. He fled immediately, my attacker, and I couldn't see for the tears that came when my nose hit the fountain drain. It took me years to relate these two incidents, my tripping Jack and then this mysterious and unwitting avenger smashing my face into the drain. Everything that goes around comes around.

I wiped the water and tears from my face and, now doubly humiliated, trudged on, down the long hall and up the stairs to the main floor and Mrs. Snodgrass's office, which was located just to the right of the front door to the school. I went quietly inside the waiting room and sat down in one of the chairs ringing the wall, and I waited. There was no secretary, only the waiting room filled with chairs for criminals like me or—even worse—parents. I waited until the tumult inside me had subsided enough that I could hear again, both the noises in the building and the automobiles going by outside. It was not too long before I realized that Mrs. Snodgrass was not in her office.

I rose and crossed to her door and carefully peered inside. No one at the desk; no one inside, hidden by the forward wall. No one home. I stepped right to the edge of the invisible barrier of the threshold. Nothing happened. So I stepped through. Still nothing. I crossed to the principal's desk, brushing my fingers lightly along the forward edge of it. I moved cautiously around the desk, to my left, trailing my fingers now along the side edge of it.

Then I was behind the desk. I twirled Mrs. Snodgrass's chair to the side and sat down in it. And there I was, a ten-year-old war criminal, sitting in the principal's chair, looking out toward the waiting room, through that door and the waiting room itself, and into the main entrance hall of our proud old school.

But even that wasn't enough.

It's hard to keep from being bad when it's in you and in the situation. Sins must pile upon sins until at last the conscience of even a deviant such as I must cry *Enough!* (Still waiting.) I opened the top drawer of the great desk before me, spied and scooped out all in one act, without a thought, a handful of the many pens and pencils I saw before me, slammed the drawer shut, rose from the chair, ran around the desk and out of the office, out the front door of the school, down the steps and gone, heading east toward Falls Church. I ran so hard, so fast, so long, that I was afraid my heart would burst, my whole chest explode. At the main crossroads of the village I threw the handful of pens and pencils into a storm drain, slowed at last to a walk, and then drifted off the main thoroughfare. I went up behind the movie theater and sat and moped. Life was hard; it wasn't my fault. What lie would I tell my parents if they found out what I had done? Who I really was? No longer Prince Charming. Life was hard. The memory of throwing those pens and pencils into the storm drain is as clear to me right now as if the whole thing happened this morning, not almost fifty years ago.

I don't remember anything else about the remainder of my time in that class, at that school. I *do* have a clear memory of the school program that spring, and of Mrs. Lesansky asking me to please come back, please be Prince Charming and save our class presentation from certain failure. But that never happened; that was just one of my dreams.

For by March of 1948, we were on our way back home, heading toward the great Southwest where men are men and women are women, where the sun sets closer to the house, where the dust of coal smoke doesn't linger hazily over your schoolyard in the evenings, over your town, over your life.

It's no wonder I've stayed in school all these many years, with memories like that to keep me going. Who wouldn't have? All I've done is move from one side of the desk to the other.

But what is it all for? Why do I remember virtually nothing I was supposed to have learned in class but remember instead only the friends I had and, even more, my run-ins with the law?

I think the answer comes in two parts.

The first is that the only true, real, sure-enough matter we are supposed to get out of public schools is how to read and write and do basic arithmetic. Anything else is gravy.

Second, the primary function of our public schools is to widen and complete the process of acculturation begun—one hopes—in the home. In other words, the schools' job is to make sure we get in the box, learn not to make waves, speak only when spoken to, raise our hands to ask permission . . . in short, to learn the social agreements. This function of the school is, in still other words, to break us, like horses are broken to the bridle and the saddle, like psychiatric patients are broken to the couch, like soldiers, through basic training, are broken to the discipline and rules of military service.

Most of us do learn how to read a little, make our mark at the bottom of a check, figure sums enough to fill out the check. And most of us learn to get in the box, too. It may take a while for the lesson to settle, but generally the process works, acculturation takes place: generally we get in the box. If we don't, we suffer.

And, for the good of society, we must. For the good of society, its rules must ultimately override the desires of the individuals who compose the society, for otherwise the society would not cohere; otherwise, there would be no society.

But, of course, we can still *think* whatever we want to. They can't take that away from us. And we must conform only if we want to get along. We do not have to; we do not have to get along. But it will cost us if we don't. If we want to, we can trip Jack into the potbellied stove, in other words, blazing with coal on a freezing winter day. But if we do, we won't get to be Prince Charming.

JOHN H. IRSFELD is a Texan whose trilogy of novels set in his native state—*Coming Through* (1975), *Little Kingdoms* (1976), and *Rats Alley* (1987)—has earned him a distinguished position in Western American letters. He now lives in Las Vegas, where he has served as academic vice president and executive assistant to the president of the University of Nevada, Las Vegas, and continues his career as a writer.

"I was fascinated by dead children and the aftermath of their passing. I think it all perhaps began in 1940 when we moved into an apartment that was annexed to a funeral parlor."

FUNERAL CHILD

RICHARD BRAUTIGAN

As a child I was very interested when other children died. There was no doubt about it that I was a morbid kid, and when other children died it always fanned the flames of my forensic curiosity.

Later, in February of 1948, this curiosity would become a personal reality and engulf and turn my life upside down and inside out like *Alice in Wonderland* taking place in a cemetery with the white rabbit as an undertaker and Alice wearing a grave-eaten shroud to play her games in.

But even in my life before that was to happen I was fascinated by dead children and the aftermath of their passing. I think it all perhaps began in 1940 when we moved into an apartment that was annexed to a funeral parlor.

The apartment had once been a functioning part of the mortuary. I don't know exactly what part, but the undertaker, to get a little extra cash, had changed the former dead space of his funeral parlor into an apartment, where we lived for a few months in the late spring of 1940.

I used to get up in the mornings and watch the funerals out the window. I had to stand on a chair because I was five years old and I wanted a good view.

I seem to remember they held some funerals early in the morning—everybody would still be asleep in the apartment and I would be wearing my pajamas.

To get at the funerals I had to roll up a window shade that was particularly difficult for my dexterity to handle. But somehow I managed it and then pulled a chair over and stood on top of it and watched the funerals.

We moved into the apartment late one afternoon, and the next morning while everybody was still asleep, I got up and wandered into the front room. I looked sleepily under the window shade and there was my first funeral, as big as death.

The hearse was parked maybe thirty feet away. Can you imagine how big that hearse seemed? That's very close for a hearse to be to a five-year-old. It seemed to me to be the size of a movie that for some very strange reason they had painted black.

That's when I first went and got the chair and pulled the window shade up after quite a struggle and moved the chair into a very good funeral-viewing position and climbed on top of it.

I did this all very quietly because I didn't want to wake anybody up in the house. Adults always like to disrupt what kids are doing, no matter what it is except if it's something the kid doesn't like. If the kid doesn't like it, the adults will let him keep on doing it forever, but if the kid likes it . . .

The hearse was filled with flowers.

There were so many flowers in the hearse that ever since then flowers have always made me feel uneasy. I like flowers, but sometimes I feel uncomfortable being in their presence. I've never let this discomfort get out of control, but I've had it ever since that morning in 1940 when I watched my first funeral.

For a while the hearse and all its flowers were just standing there alone except for two men dressed in black who seemed not to be in a hurry, just waiting. They could almost have been flowers themselves: some kind of black daffodils.

One of them was smoking a cigarette. He had smoked it down so short that it looked as if the butt were going to set his hand on fire. The other one kept stroking a long, very black mustache that looked as if it had jumped off the hearse and right onto his face, but that didn't seem to bother him.

You probably want to know how I knew I was watching a funeral if I was only five years old and I had never seen this sort of thing before and nobody had told me about such goings-on. The answer to this is very simple: I saw one in the movies, just a week before, and figured it out for myself.

After a while the two men who were waiting beside the hearse went into the funeral parlor and then people started coming out. The people were all very somber and moved appropriately. They seemed to be in slow motion. Though I was close to them, standing on my chair, it was difficult to hear what they were saying.

This was becoming very interesting.

I could hardly wait to see what would happen next.

The two men in black came back out with some other men, carrying the coffin. They put it in the back of the hearse. Actually, they had to sort of stuff it in because of all the flowers, but somehow they managed it and the two men got into the front seat where the living traveled.

The mourners walked very s l o w l y and started getting into parked cars. The cars all had one-word signs on their windshields, but I didn't know what the word said. It would be years before I figured it out.

Pretty soon everybody was gone and the street was very quiet in the wake of their departure. The first thing I heard after they were gone was a bird singing just outside the window.

I got down from the chair and went back to my bed. I lay there staring at the ceiling and digesting what I had just seen. I stayed in bed until everybody else woke up.

When I heard them moving around in the kitchen, I got up and joined them. They were still sleepy and making some coffee to begin the war of another day.

They asked me if I'd had a good night's sleep.

For an unknown reason I pondered their question, which really didn't even need a reply. I mean, I could have said any little thing and that would have been okay, but I stood there, thinking hard about it.

They continued what they were already doing and immediately forgot that they had asked me something. People aren't really interested for any length of time if a five-year-old had a good night's sleep, and that's what was happening to me.

"Yes, I did," I finally said.

"Did what?" they asked.

"Had a good night's sleep."

"Oh," they said, looking at me curiously because they had forgotten what they had asked me. Adults are always doing that with children.

Anyway, I got up early and watched the funerals after that. There of course wasn't a funeral every morning, and I was disappointed when there wasn't one. I went back to bed and hoped that there would be a funeral the next morning.

There were other funerals going on during the day, but I didn't care about them very much.

I was strictly a morning funeral child.

RICHARD BRAUTIGAN, a native of Washington, became perhaps the most innovative and admired young American writer of the 1960s and '70s. In books like *Trout Fishing in America* and *A Confederate General from Big Sur* he helped reinvent how authors viewed and recreated their worlds. This piece is an excerpt from his autobiography, *So the Wind Won't Blow It All Away* (1982).

"Ragtag bits of this and that he had touched, stacked, stored. Useless to anyone but him, and he's gone now."

ELEGY

JAMES D. HOUSTON

At the county dump I am throwing away my father. His old paint rags, and stumps of brushes. Color charts. The spattered leather suitcase he used for so many years to carry the small tools and tiny jars of his trade, a suitcase so cracked and bent and buckle-ripped it's no good for anything now. I start to toss it on top of the brushes and rags, but hold back.

I toss instead the five-gallon drums that once held primer. He stacked them against one wall of his shop, for no good reason, kept dozens more than he would ever use. Around these I toss the bottles and tubes from his medicine chest. And cracked boots, filled with dust, as if in his closet it has been raining dust for years. And magazines. His fishing hat. Notes to himself:

Fix Window

Grease car

Call Harlow about job.

Bent nails in a jar, rolls of old wire, pipe sections, a fiddle he always intended to mend, old paid bills, check stubs, pencils his teeth chewed. Ragtag bits of this and that he had touched, stacked, stored. Useless to anyone but him, and he's gone now.

So I toss it all out there among the refrigerators and lettuce leaves, truck tires, busted sofas, and flowerpots. Onto that heap I throw my father, saving for the last that suitcase of his I'd first seen twenty years back—and it was old then—that day he took me out on a job for the first time, wearing a pair of his spattered overalls, rolled thick at the cuff, and a Sherwin-Williams white billcap.

"What're ya gonna do, Dad?" I say that first morning.

He doesn't answer. He never answers, as if he prefers silence. And I always wait, as if each silence is an exception, and this time he will turn and speak. It's my big reason for coming along this morning, the chance that out here on the job something might pass between us. I would never have been able to describe it ahead of time, but . . . maybe . . . something.

I wait and watch. Two minutes of puckering lips and long, slow blinks while he studies the labels, then he selects one tube, unscrews its top, and squeezes out a little on his fingertips.

I follow him to the five-gallon drum he's mixing paint in. A short stick of plywood holds the color he's shooting for—pale, pale green. He's proud of his eye for color, his knack for figuring just how pale this green will be when it dries. I watch and learn. Squeeze a green strip from the tube and stir it in, wide easy stirs while the green spirals out. Stir and stir. Then test: dip another stick in. Check the color. Stir.

"Okay, Jim. Take half this green paint and get that wall there covered."

He hands me a clean brush. Its black bristles shine with yesterday's thinner. He pours a gallon bucket full of paint for me and cuts the fall off clean.

"I'll be back in a minute," he says.

It's the first time I've painted anything away from home. I do not yet know that before summer is out I will dread the look of any long unpainted wall and wince at the smell of paint and thinner. But now I want this one to be a good job. I want to live up to the paint my dad has just mixed. I start by the living room door, taking my time, keeping the molding clear for a white trim later.

Ten minutes pass, and this first wall becomes my world. I am moving across the wide-open country—working my brush like Dad told me to, using the wrist, lapping strokes over—when I feel the need to turn around.

In the far doorway, the lady of the house stands glaring at me with a look of shock and anger. Next to the wall of her priceless living room she finds a kid dressed up in his father's overalls with the cuffs rolled thick. I realize how dangerous I look to her. Under my new green freckles my face turns scarlet.

The woman is gone.

From the hallway I hear her loud whisper. "Mr. Houston! That boy painting my living room couldn't be over fifteen!"

"He's thirteen, Ma'am."

"He's what?"

"It's my boy, Jim. He's giving me a hand this summer."

"I just wonder if he knows what he's doing in there."

"I painted my first house when I was ten."

"Well . . . I . . . if . . . I'd certainly be keeping an eye on him if I were you."

"Don't worry, Ma'am, he knows what to do."

Behind me I hear her walking slowly across the room. I keep painting; I don't look at her this time. Put plenty of paint on the brush. But don't let it run. Feather it at the overlap. Cover. Cover.

Dad comes in and fills up another gallon bucket and helps me finish the wall. He catches my eye once and winks. Then we are painting toward each other in a silence broken only by the whish of bristles and the cluck of brush handle against the can. Somewhere in the back of the house a radio is playing its faraway music.

We finish the room by quitting time. Dad looks over my work, finds a couple of bald spots along the baseboard, and has me fill these in, saying only, "Keep an eye out for them holidays." We clean the brushes. He drops the lid shut on his kit of a suitcase, snaps the buckle to, straps it, and says, "Might as well take that on out to the truck."

I had never paid much attention to his kit. Now I know just enough about what's inside for it to be mysterious. A year from now I will know too much about what's inside. By then I will be able to read his half smile, his apology for having only this to offer me. But today carrying it is an honor. No one has ever carried that kit but him. It has a manly weight, a fine weight for carrying from the house to the curb, for hoisting onto the truck bed. It lands with a *thunk* and sits solid.

I wait for Dad to tie his ladder on the overhead rack, and we climb into the cab. He winks once more as we prepare to leave Mrs. So-and-so behind. Reeking of paint and turpentine, we are Sherwin and Williams calling it a day, with no way to talk much over the rattle of his metal-floored Chevy, and no need to talk. The clutch leaps. Wind rushes in, mixing paint and gasoline fumes, and all you need to do is to stay loose for the jolts and the whole long rumble ride home.

At the county dump, I am throwing away my father, lifting his old suitcase to toss the last of him onto the smoking heap. It is crusted with splats of seventy colors now, its lid corners split as if somebody sat on it. The ragged straps dangle. One shred of leather holds the chromium buckle that still catches the sun where the paint doesn't cover it. The shred of leather gives. The buckle breaks. The kit flies open.

As if compressed inside, waiting to escape, the smell of oil and pigment cuts through the smoke and rot that fills the air around me. My throwing arm stays. My other hand reaches out. I'm holding the suitcase, inhaling the smell that always clung to him, even after he had scrubbed. It rose from the creases in his hands, from the white lines rimming his fingernails, from the paint specks he sometimes missed with the thinner at the corners of his eyes. I breath it in deep.

I close the suitcase slowly, prepare to heave it once and for all. This time with both hands, out and up. Out among all those things you find only by losing them.

One last glance. By five tonight this, too, will be gone for good, when the bulldozer comes to shove it over the side with the rest of today's collection—treasures of yesterday, old necessities, parts of the heart.

JAMES D. HOUSTON is one of the many outstanding authors who studied with Wallace Stegner at Stanford. He was born and raised in California of Southwestern migrant parents—"Okies"—and his work illustrates a strong bond with nature and landscapes. Houston's fiction includes *Continental Drift* (1978), *The Automotive Adventures of Charlie Bates* (1978), and *Love Life* (1985), as well as *Farewell to Manzanar* (1973), which he co-wrote with his wife, Jeanne Wakatsuki Houston. They have three children.

EPILOGUE: WHO WE ARE

MAREK BREIGER

The Mexican music plays, the accordion and guitars and horns, and the plaintive male singer is joined by the soft voices of women on the chorus.

Tortillas are being ground and pounded.

I am on Mission Boulevard, across from Moreau High School, where I've taught English for more than ten years. I am at La Casa Latina, drinking coffee, reading and writing.

On the street, a family walks past, the mother wearing a shawl, followed by her four children. The oldest, a girl, pushes a baby carriage: the soulful dark eyes of Mexico define her face.

Inside, in broken English, a man asks his wife

"Pine Yapple? or Dijet Pepsi?"

He speaks in the accent so easy to parody but that only fools mock, for he speaks the broken English that novelist Wright Morris once described as "the language of the soul, broken words, spoken to the heart."

Construction workers come in for an early lunch of beer and tortillas, easily mixing Spanish and American slang.

Everything is orderly. Everyone is polite in the Latin

tradition, and I am not treated as a stranger—and perhaps I am not. For I am viewing an American and a Mexican scene and more.

I am viewing immigrant America, the America my Russian Jewish grandparents found on the west side of Chicago and the Lower East Side of New York and in Boyle Heights in Los Angeles.

It is the America of old country emotion and new country language and hope.

A taped sign, dark ink on white paper states, "Velodores, Candles, 12 × 15," and I think of the Yarzheit, the memorial candle lit for my sister Miriam, for Mimi, every January 26.

What a price we pay when we give up the emotional language of the immigrants—our parents, grandparents, and great-grandparents.

Across the street, at the high school, for more than ten years, I've tried to teach the work of authors—writers such as Hemingway and Steinbeck, Elie Wiesel and Chief Seattle, Studs Terkel and Martin Luther King—who protested against our collective loss of memory and sense of justice.

For we Americans are a nation of immigrants and minority groups. We are not merely "whites," but Italian and Armenian and Irish and Spanish and German and Portuguese and Greek and Polish and all of the rest. We are not simply "people of color," but West African Ashanti and Filipino and Japanese and Chinese and Korean and Pakistani and Cambodian and Ohlone Indian and all of the rest.

We have yet to learn a simple lesson—putting down or pre-judging others because of race or religion is not an act of celebration or pride or an effective act of retribution: it is an act that works to divide and to make real progress impossible.

The accordion plays, the words are sung, the man behind the counter joins in and seems to remember a different time.

And outside it is still morning and there is no school and cars move past a scene of Hayward, of Northern California, and of the world.

MAREK BREIGER, who teaches English at Moreau High School in Hayward, California, is also a columnist for *California English,* as well as an active freelance writer.

CREDITS

Previously Unpublished

ABOUT THE EDITORS

Alexandra Haslam and Gerald Haslam are daughter and father, as well as pals. She was a longtime editor of *BAM* magazine and is now a free-lance writer and editor. From her mother, Alex adds Cree, French, Polish, and German to her father's ethnic mix—Irish, English, Portuguese, Welsh, Sephardic, Danish, Spanish—a California version of *la raza cósmica*. Gerry is the author of seven collections of short stories, most recently *Condor Dreams* (1994), a novel, three essay collections, and several other books of nonfiction. He has also edited four previous anthologies. Both now live in rural northern California. Both are—or were—athletes. Alex has a sister, three brothers, and a boyfriend. Gerry has one wife, Alex's mother.